A Five Ingredient Cookbook

by Debbye Dabbs

Take Five
A Holiday Cookbook

Quick and Easy Holiday Food

Take Five, A Holiday Cookbook
Published by D.D. Publishing
Copyright © 2003 Debbye Dabbs
117 Muscadine Hill
Madison, Mississippi 39110
601-856-4037

Library of Congress Number: 2003092916
ISBN: 0-9645899-5-8

Edited, designed, and manufactured by Favorite Recipes® Press
an imprint of

FRP™

2451 Atrium Way
Nashville, Tennessee 37214
1-800-358-0560

Book Design: Brad Whitfield & Susan Breining
Art Director: Steve Newman
Managing Editor: Mary Cummings
Project Editor: Judy Jackson

Manufactured in the United States of America
First Printing: 2003   20,000 copies
Second Printing: 2004   16,000 copies

Acknowledgments

This book is dedicated to my husband, who encouraged me
and helped me meet all of my deadlines.
Thank you, Kelly, for testing all the recipes found in this book.
Also, a special thanks to my neighbors who helped with
the tasting and sampling—and even rated the recipes
and voted for their favorites!

Also, a very special thanks to my children, my grandson,
and my parents for their prayers and support.

Take Five, A Holiday Cookbook is also dedicated
to my grandmother, who taught me to love the holidays
and showed me the true meaning of the Christmas season.
Happy cooking!

Debbye Dabbs

"We love Him, because He first loved us."
1 John 4:19

Foreword

The kids are running with riotous abandon in the hallway.
The dog is out, yet again. And your dinner guests are on their way.
Don't panic. Just "Take Five."

Designed to make your life easier and more enjoyable,
Debbye Dabbs's Take Five cookbook series is the break you've been
looking for. With no more than five ingredients in each recipe,
its simplicity is its charm.

It all started in 1993 with *Take Five, A Cookbook*. Encouraged by
her husband and two children, Dabbs self-published this first book,
which is now in its fourteenth printing. It has been printed in Braille,
too, and adopted by the Mississippi School for the Blind.

The following year, in 1994, *Take Five, A Light Cookbook*,
was published. And in 1996, her third book, *Take Five, A Christmas
Cookbook*, put everyone in the Christmas spirit. She crossed the
gender barrier with *Beyond the Grill, A Cookbook for Men*,
published in 1997, and she served up a winning combination in
her *Take Five for Every Occasion*, published in 2000.

That's right! Dabbs bridges the generation gap with recipes
the kids will beg to make again and again. Just leave
the delicious details up to Dabbs. She takes care of it all—
from the men to the children and all the parties in between.
So, add a dash of simplicity to the complexities of life and
Take Five from the clutter.

Adrienne Stewart Patton

Contents

Take 5... Menus of Winter

Christmas Eve Carols and Candlelight

- - - -

Breakfast with Santa

- - - -

Old-Fashioned Christmas Dinner

Holiday Open House

- - - - -

New Year's Eve Buffet

- - - - -

"Be My Valentine" Supper

- - - - -

Fast-Lane Dinners for Winter

Sally's Tomato Basil Bisque

2 (10-ounce) cans tomato soup
1 (14-ounce) can diced tomatoes
2¹/₂ cups buttermilk
3 tablespoons chopped fresh basil
¹/₄ teaspoon freshly ground pepper

Combine the undiluted soup, tomatoes, buttermilk and basil in a 3-quart saucepan. Cook over medium heat for 6 to 9 minutes, stirring frequently. Ladle into soup bowls. Season each serving with pepper.

Yield: 6 servings

- - - -

The tomatoes can be mashed with a fork or processed in a blender for 2 minutes to make a smoother soup.

Spinach Blue Cheese Salad

1 bag fresh baby spinach leaves
1 cup pecans, chopped
1 large apple, thinly sliced
1/2 cup crumbled blue cheese
1/2 cup bottled oil and vinegar salad dressing

Place the spinach in a large salad bowl. Add the pecans, apple and cheese and toss to mix. Add the dressing and toss gently to coat.

Yield: 4 servings

Make your table say "Merry Christmas." Save the brown paper rolls that hold wrapping paper or paper towels. Cut them into 6-inch pieces. Fill them with small gifts and wrap in red or green paper. Use gold or silver ribbon to tie the end of each roll. (They should look like a kid's party favor.) Place them above each plate.

Shrimp Etouffée

2 bags frozen mixed onions, bell peppers and celery
2 (10-ounce) cans chicken broth (not low sodium)
1 (16-ounce) jar home-style chicken gravy
1 cup home-style pasta sauce
2 pounds fresh shrimp, steamed spicy (see Note)

Place the frozen vegetables in a large skillet. Pour 1 can of the chicken broth over the vegetables. Simmer for 15 minutes, stirring occasionally. Add the gravy, pasta sauce and remaining chicken broth. Peel the shrimp and add to the skillet. Simmer for 20 minutes, stirring occasionally. Serve over saffron rice.
Note: Most supermarkets will steam shrimp at no charge.

Yield: 8 servings

■ ■ ■ ■

In this recipe, the prepared chicken gravy becomes a basic roux. This festive entrée is even better made a day in advance.

Glazed Carrots

1 medium bunch carrots, peeled and sliced
2 tablespoons butter
$1/3$ cup packed brown sugar
$1/2$ teaspoon nutmeg
$1/4$ cup fresh orange juice

Cook the carrots in water to cover in a saucepan until tender; drain. Combine the cooked carrots, butter, brown sugar, nutmeg and orange juice in the saucepan. Cook until heated through, stirring until the carrots are glazed.

Yield: 4 servings

For Christmas in a Mug, combine 2 cups cranberry juice, 2 cups apple juice, and 5 cloves in a small saucepan, and simmer for 10 to 12 minutes. Strain into mugs, discarding the cloves. Your home will smell like Christmas, and you can serve your family a wonderful, warm drink.

Even Better the Next Day Cake

1 (2-layer) package butter-recipe yellow cake mix
1 (14-ounce) can sweetened condensed milk
1 (20-ounce) can crushed pineapple in juice
16 ounces whipped topping
1 cup flaked coconut

Prepare and bake the cake mix using the package directions for a 9×13-inch cake pan. Poke holes in the top of the cake. Mix the condensed milk and undrained pineapple in a bowl and pour over the cake. Top with the whipped topping. Sprinkle evenly with the coconut. Chill until serving time.

Yield: 12 servings

- - - -

Another favorite cake starting with a time-saving cake mix!

Caroline's Cheese Torte

2 eggs, beaten
1 (4-ounce) can chopped green chiles
16 ounces Monterey Jack cheese with jalapeño chiles
2 tablespoons flour
$1/3$ cup milk

Combine the eggs, green chiles, cheese, flour and milk in a bowl and mix well. Pour into a greased 8×10-inch baking dish. Bake at 350 degrees for 35 minutes. Let cool before cutting into squares.

Yield: 10 servings

- - - -

A holiday breakfast during the week is a great way to get mothers with young children together. This is also a great way to entertain busy friends and neighbors.

Watt's Christmas Casserole

5 slices bread, cut into cubes
1 pound sausage, browned and drained
1 cup (4 ounces) shredded Cheddar cheese
6 eggs, beaten
2 cups milk

Place the bread cubes in a greased 9×13-inch baking pan.
Mix the sausage, cheese, eggs and milk in a bowl and spoon into
the baking pan. Bake at 350 degrees for 35 minutes.

Yield: 10 servings

*This is a perfect breakfast to serve to
your overnight guests.*

Freddie's Cheesy Grits

1 1/2 cups grits
1/2 cup (1 stick) butter
1 pound Velveeta cheese, shredded
3 eggs, beaten
1/2 cup milk

Cook the grits using the package directions. Combine the cooked grits, butter, cheese, eggs and milk in a bowl and mix well. Spoon into a greased baking dish. Bake at 325 degrees for 1 hour.

Yield: 8 servings

- - - -

On a sunny weekend morning, place a quilt over your patio table and serve your family breakfast outside.

Stacy's Fruit Bowl

1 (21-ounce) can peach pie filling
1 (8-ounce) can pineapple chunks, drained
2 or 3 bananas, chopped
1 (10-ounce) package frozen strawberries, thawed and drained
1 (11-ounce) can mandarin oranges, drained

Combine the pie filling, pineapple, bananas, strawberries
and oranges in a bowl and mix well. Chill thoroughly before serving.

Yield: 6 to 8 servings

----

*If you place your Christmas tree in a corner, be
sure to tie it so that it won't fall. Place small wrapped
packages into the tree to fill any holes.*

Fran's Monkey Bread

24 frozen Parker House rolls, thawed

3/4 cup (1 1/2 sticks) margarine, melted

1 1/2 cups sugar

3 tablespoons cinnamon

1 cup chopped pecans

Cut each roll into 3 pieces. Mix the melted margarine, sugar and cinnamon in a bowl. Dip each roll into the margarine mixture. Place in an ungreased tube pan. Sprinkle the pecans over the rolls. Let rise for 2 hours. Bake at 350 degrees for 40 minutes.

Yield: 12 servings

Parker House rolls were made famous by a Boston hotel of that name.

Shelton Cheese Biscuits

1 cup (2 sticks) butter, melted
8 ounces sharp Cheddar cheese, shredded
1 egg, beaten
$1/4$ teaspoon cayenne pepper
1 loaf thinly sliced white bread, crusts removed

Beat the butter, cheese, egg and cayenne pepper in a mixing bowl until fluffy. Stack 3 bread slices together. Spread the cheese mixture between each slice and over the top and sides of the stack. Repeat with the remaining ingredients. Place on greased baking sheets. Bake at 350 degrees for 12 minutes.

Yield: 6 to 8 servings

- - - -

*Eggs should be stored in their carton
in the refrigerator.*

Apple Pumpkin Cake

1 (2-layer) package spice cake mix
1/2 cup water
3 eggs
1 cup applesauce
1 (15-ounce) can pumpkin

Combine the cake mix, water and eggs in a mixing bowl
and mix well. Add the applesauce and pumpkin and mix well.
Spoon into a 9×13-inch cake pan. Bake at 350 degrees
for 30 to 35 minutes or until a wooden pick inserted near the
center comes out clean. Cool in the pan.

Yield: 12 servings

- - - -

*A sweet treat for breakfast or tucked
into a lunchbox.*

Cinnamon Spiced Cider

1 gallon apple cider
1 cup red hot cinnamon candies
1 orange, thinly sliced
2 tablespoons frozen lemonade concentrate

Combine the cider, candies, orange slices and lemonade concentrate in a large stockpot. Bring to a boil; reduce the heat. Simmer for 30 minutes. Serve hot.

Yield: 16 to 20 servings

– – – –

Use small silver jingle bells strung on a thin wire to form holiday napkin rings. (Kids will love this project!)

Lott's Christmas Salad

3 cups water
1 (6-ounce) package raspberry gelatin
2 (16-ounce) cans whole berry cranberry sauce
8 ounces cream cheese
1/2 cup pecan chips

Bring the water to a boil in a large saucepan. Add the gelatin, stirring until dissolved. Add the cranberry sauce and mix well. Pour into a 9×13-inch dish. Cut the cream cheese into 16 cubes. Shape into balls and roll in the pecan chips. Place 2 inches apart on top of the gelatin. Press each into the gelatin with the back of a spoon. Chill for 2 hours before serving.

Yield: 6 to 8 servings

— — — —

Help your children make Christmas and birthday gifts for relatives. (Grandparents will be thrilled!)

Traditional Turkey

1 (20-pound) frozen turkey, thawed
2 tablespoons vegetable oil
2 tablespoons salt
1 tablespoon pepper
1 tablespoon chopped fresh parsley

Remove the giblets and neck from the turkey cavity; reserve for making giblet gravy if desired. Coat the turkey with the vegetable oil. Sprinkle half the salt and pepper inside the turkey. Sprinkle the remaining salt and pepper and the parsley over the turkey. Place in a roasting pan and cover with foil. Bake at 350 degrees for $4^{1}/2$ hours. Remove the foil and bake for 15 minutes longer or until brown and cooked through. (Turkey is done when a meat thermometer inserted into its thickest portion registers 180 degrees.)

Yield: 12 servings

■ ■ ■ ■

Use your paper shredder to make your own confetti . . . bright colors for spring, red and green for Christmas, and so forth.

Sweet Potato Casserole

2 (23-ounce) cans sweet potatoes, drained and mashed
3 eggs
1 cup (2 sticks) butter
1 cup packed brown sugar
1 cup pecans, chopped

Combine the sweet potatoes, eggs, half the butter and half the brown sugar in a bowl and mix well. Spoon into a greased 9×13-inch baking dish. Top with a mixture of the remaining butter and brown sugar. Sprinkle with the pecans. Bake at 350 degrees for 30 minutes.

Yield: 8 servings

- - - -

Make Corn Bread Dressing by cooking 4 cups chicken broth and 1 1/2 cups chopped onions in a saucepan for 15 minutes. Mix with 4 cups crumbled corn bread, 6 cups torn bread pieces, and 6 beaten eggs. Spoon into a 9×13-inch baking dish, and bake at 400 degrees for 35 minutes. Makes 8 servings.

Asparagus Amandine

2 cups bread crumbs
2 cups (8 ounces) shredded sharp Cheddar cheese
2 (15-ounce) cans asparagus tips, drained
6 ounces blanched sliced almonds
1 (10-ounce) can cream of mushroom soup

Mix the bread crumbs and cheese together. Sprinkle $1/3$ of the mixture in a greased casserole. Layer the asparagus, almonds, undiluted soup and remaining cheese mixture $1/2$ at a time in the casserole, ending with the cheese mixture. Bake at 350 degrees for 30 minutes or until heated through and brown on top.

Yield: 6 to 8 servings

■ ■ ■ ■

Asparagus was considered a luxury in ancient Greece and Rome.

Chess Pie

1^1/$_2$ **cups sugar**
^{3}/$_4$ **cup (1^1/$_2$ sticks) butter**
2 tablespoons cornmeal
1 tablespoon vinegar
3 eggs

Combine the sugar, butter, cornmeal, vinegar and eggs
in a bowl and mix well. Pour into an unbaked 9-inch pie shell.
Bake at 350 degrees for 30 minutes.

Yield: 6 to 8 servings

- - - -

*Cakes and pies make beautiful holiday centerpieces.
Use a glass dome over a Christmas plate to show
off your favorite dessert!*

Toffee Trifle

6 large deli brownies
6 (4-ounce) packages chocolate pudding mix, prepared
8 ounces whipped topping
6 toffee candy bars, crushed

Place 3 brownies in a trifle bowl or other transparent glass bowl. Layer the pudding, whipped topping and candy crumbs $1/2$ at a time over the brownies. Top with the remaining brownies. Chill, covered, overnight.

Yield: 10 servings

For a bridal luncheon, use old family silver cups, bowls, and small pitchers to hold fresh flowers. For example, an old silver baby cup becomes a miniature vase for spray roses.

Frozen Banana Punch

1 (12-ounce) can frozen lemonade concentrate
3 cups water
3 bananas, mashed
4 cups pineapple juice
1 (1-liter) bottle ginger ale

Mix the lemonade concentrate and water in a large freezer-proof container. Stir in the bananas and pineapple juice. Freeze until firm. Let stand at room temperature for 1 hour before serving. Stir in the ginger ale just before serving.

Yield: 20 servings

- - - -

The fresh bananas in this cool, refreshing punch add a tasty twist.

Meeting Street Crab Dip

1 (8-ounce) container French onion dip
8 ounces cream cheese, softened
1/4 cup lemon juice
Cayenne pepper to taste
1 (7-ounce) can crab meat, drained and flaked

Combine the onion dip, cream cheese, lemon juice and cayenne pepper in a bowl and mix well. Stir in the crab meat. Serve with crackers.

Yield: 12 servings

— — —

Did you know that your own backyard contains almost everything you need to "deck the halls" for Christmas? Fresh pine boughs, magnolia leaves, holly berries, apples, and fresh lemons can be placed around a punch bowl to decorate your home for the holidays.

Hot Crawfish Dip

4 green onions, chopped
$1/2$ cup (1 stick) butter
24 ounces cream cheese, cut into cubes
2 (12-ounce) packages frozen crawfish tails, thawed and drained
2 teaspoons red pepper flakes

Sauté the green onions in the butter in a skillet. Reduce the heat and add the cream cheese. Cook until the cream cheese is melted, stirring frequently. Stir in the crawfish tails and pepper flakes. Serve hot with melba toast rounds.

Yield: 50 servings

- - - -

Crawfish tails can be found in the frozen food section of most supermarkets.

Hot Cheddar Dip

3 cups (12 ounces) shredded Cheddar cheese
1 cup mayonnaise
1 cup chopped onion
1 teaspoon crushed red pepper

Combine the cheese, mayonnaise, onion and red pepper
in a bowl and mix well. Spoon into a 1$1/2$-quart round baking dish.
Bake at 350 degrees for 10 to 12 minutes or just until bubbly.
Broil for 1 to 2 minutes or until light brown.

Yield: 8 to 10 servings

■ ■ ■ ■

*To keep your Christmas tree fresh, add a can
of lemon-lime carbonated beverage and 2 aspirin to
the water in the tree stand.*

Jennie's Spinach Dip

1 (10-ounce) package frozen spinach, thawed and drained
1/2 cup (1 stick) butter, melted
1 onion, chopped
1 cup heavy cream
6 ounces fresh Parmesan cheese, grated

Mix the spinach, butter and onion in a bowl. Stir in the cream gradually. Fold in the cheese. Spoon into a medium baking dish. Bake at 350 degrees for 25 minutes.

Yield: 8 servings

▬ ▬ ▬ ▬

Kids love to help wrap gifts, so save old newspapers, brown bags, and recycled paper for them to use as wrapping paper. Tie the packages with colorful green or red ribbons.

Mushroom Puffs

8 ounces cream cheese, softened
1 (4-ounce) can mushrooms, drained and chopped
2 green onions, chopped
1 teaspoon seasoned salt
2 (8-count) cans refrigerator crescent rolls

Mix the cream cheese, mushrooms, green onions and seasoned salt in a bowl. Unroll both cans of crescent roll dough and shape each into a rectangle. Press the perforations to seal. Spread half the cream cheese mixture over each rectangle. Roll up each rectangle as for a jelly roll and cut into 1-inch slices. Place on a baking sheet. Bake at 375 degrees for 10 minutes. Serve hot.

Yield: 48 servings

Start a gift closet or gift drawer. After each season, buy small gifts on clearance (sometimes holiday items are reduced by 75%). Keep them in your gift closet, and you'll be ahead of the rush next year.

Chocolate Pecan Toffee

35 saltine crackers
1 cup packed brown sugar
1 cup (2 sticks) butter or margarine
2 cups (12 ounces) semisweet chocolate chips, melted
1/2 cup chopped pecans

Line a 10×15-inch baking sheet with foil. Cover with the crackers. Boil the brown sugar and butter in a saucepan for 3 minutes. Pour over the crackers. Bake at 350 degrees for 5 minutes. Spread the chocolate over the top and sprinkle with the pecans. Place in the freezer for fast cooling, and then break up into chunks.

Yield: 48 servings

- - - -

Nuts will last for six to nine months if stored in the refrigerator.

Microwave Fudge

3 cups (18 ounces) milk chocolate chips
1 (14-ounce) can sweetened condensed milk
1/4 cup (1/2 stick) butter or margarine, cut into pieces

Combine the chocolate chips, condensed milk and butter in a 2-quart microwave-safe glass bowl. Microwave on Medium (50% power) for 5 minutes, stirring after 2 minutes. Pour into a greased 8×8-inch dish. Chill, covered, for 8 hours. Cut into squares to serve. Store in the refrigerator.

Yield: 36 pieces

- - - -

Make this candy for your school's next bake sale and be the first to sell out!

Chocolate Chip Truffles

1 roll refrigerator chocolate chip cookie dough
2 pounds white almond bark
1 square (1 ounce) dark chocolate
2 cups (12 ounces) chocolate chips

Shape the cookie dough into 1-inch balls and freeze until firm. Turn a slow cooker on High. Combine the almond bark, dark chocolate and chocolate chips in the slow cooker, stirring until melted. Dip the frozen balls into the melted chocolate. Place on waxed paper to harden. Store in the refrigerator.

Yield: 48 pieces

- - - -

If you have leftover melted chocolate, dip pretzels or store-bought cookies in it to give them a festive holiday coating.

Crunchy Candy Clusters

2 pounds white almond bark, broken into small pieces
1¹/₂ cups chunky peanut butter
4 cups Cap'n Crunch Cereal
4 cups crisp rice cereal
4 cups miniature marshmallows

Place the almond bark in a 5-quart slow cooker. Cover and cook on High for 30 minutes. Stir in the peanut butter. Add all the cereal and the marshmallows, stirring to coat. Drop by tablespoonfuls onto waxed paper.

Yield: 72 clusters

- - - -

Leave some cookies out for Santa. He will thank you later.

K. Belle Coconut Treats

1 deli angel food cake
1 can flaked coconut, finely chopped
1 (1-pound) package confectioners' sugar
1/2 cup milk

Slice off the browned part of the cake; reserve for another use. Cut the remaining cake into "fingers." Spread the coconut on a sheet of waxed paper. Mix the confectioners' sugar and milk in a bowl until the mixture is the consistency of icing. Dip the cake fingers into the icing. Roll the cake in the coconut. These freeze well.

Yield: 24 cookies

These cookies are great with a bowl of fresh fruit.

Kelly's Vegetable Dip

8 ounces cream cheese, softened
1 envelope Italian salad dressing mix
1 cup chopped green olives
1 cup sour cream

Beat the cream cheese in a mixing bowl until light and fluffy.
Add the salad dressing mix, olives and sour cream and mix well. Chill,
covered, until serving time. Serve with fresh vegetables. This dip is also
good served on fresh bread rounds topped with tomato slices.

Yield: 24 to 30 servings

---

*To make cleanup easier, line baking sheets with foil
before making toast or baking sandwiches.*

Campbell's Corn Chowder

2 (10-ounce) cans cream of potato soup
1 (15-ounce) can corn kernels
1 (12-ounce) can evaporated milk
4 chicken breasts, cooked and chopped
1/4 cup (1/2 stick) butter

Combine the undiluted soup, corn, evaporated milk, chicken and butter in a saucepan. Cook over medium heat until heated through, stirring occasionally.

Yield: 6 servings

- - - -

Visit a farmer's market or roadside vegetable stand for fresh vegetables to make this soup even more nourishing.

Pineapple Glazed Pork Tenderloin

1 teaspoon granulated or minced garlic
1 (20-ounce) can pineapple chunks
1/2 (10-ounce) bottle soy sauce
1/4 cup packed brown sugar
2 pounds pork tenderloin

Combine the garlic, undrained pineapple, soy sauce and brown sugar in a large sealable plastic bag. Add the pork. Seal the bag and turn several times to coat the pork. Chill overnight. Remove the pork from the marinade and place in a baking dish. Pour 1 inch of marinade into the baking dish; discard any remaining marinade. Bake at 350 degrees for 1 1/2 hours or until a meat thermometer inserted in the thickest portion registers 160 degrees.

Yield: 6 to 8 servings

- - - -

Grilled pork tenderloin and fresh pineapple can be arranged on a large platter with a vegetable and a starchy food. The presentation will be beautiful, and you will have only one serving plate to clean up.

Jezebel Sauce

1 (5-ounce) jar horseradish
1 (1.1-ounce) can dry mustard
1 (18-ounce) jar pineapple preserves
1 (18-ounce) jar apple jelly
1 (8-ounce) block cream cheese

Mix the horseradish and dry mustard in a small bowl. Combine with the preserves and jelly in a large bowl. Spread over the cream cheese. Serve with crackers. Note: Be sure to mix the horseradish and dry mustard togehter first to keep it from being lumpy. This sauce is also great with pork or beef.

Yield: 6 to 8 servings

- - - -

Make Horseradish Sauce by mixing 1 cup mayonnaise, 2 tablespoons horseradish, 1 teaspoon Worcestershire sauce, and Tabasco sauce to taste in a bowl. Chill until serving time. Serve with pork. Makes 1 1/4 cups.

Garlic Mashed Potatoes

5 medium potatoes, cooked, peeled and sliced
1/2 cup milk
6 tablespoons butter, melted
1 teaspoon purchased roasted garlic
1 teaspoon salt

Place the potatoes in a large mixing bowl. Add the milk, butter and garlic. Beat at medium speed for 2 to 3 minutes or until smooth. Season with the salt.

Yield: 6 servings

■ ■ ■ ■

This vegetable dish is so rich and creamy that even picky eaters will not be able to resist.

Vegetable Topper

3 tablespoons butter
3 tablespoons flour
1/2 cup half-and-half
1/4 cup white wine
1 cup (4 ounces) shredded sharp Cheddar cheese

Melt the butter in a saucepan. Stir in the flour. Stir in the half-and-half gradually. Cook until thickened and smooth, stirring constantly. Stir in the wine and cheese. Pour over vegetables of your choice.

Yield: About 2 cups

Give a party in honor of a friend or elderly parent. It will bring joy to both of you.

Miniature Oreo Cheesecakes

24 Oreo cookies
24 ounces cream cheese, softened
3/4 cup sugar
3 eggs
1 cup chocolate syrup

Line 24 muffin cups with paper liners. Place 1 cookie in each.
Beat the cream cheese and sugar in a mixing bowl
until blended and smooth. Add the eggs and beat for 2 minutes.
Spoon 1/3 cup of the mixture over each cookie. Bake at
350 degrees for 18 minutes. Chill thoroughly. Drizzle chocolate
syrup over each cheesecake just before serving.

Yield: 24 servings

----

*This is a spectacular dessert to serve
on a holiday.*

Mock Champagne Punch

1 quart apple juice
2 (1-liter) bottles ginger ale
Red food coloring

Thoroughly chill the apple juice and ginger ale. Mix the
apple juice and ginger ale in a large container just before serving.
Stir in the desired amount of food coloring.

Yield: 12 servings

- - - -

A delicious beginning for a relaxing weekend.

Sun-Dried Tomato Dip

1 (7-ounce) jar sun-dried tomatoes in oil, drained and chopped
8 ounces cream cheese, softened
$1/2$ cup sour cream
$1/2$ cup mayonnaise
Tops only of 2 green onions, chopped

Combine the tomatoes, cream cheese, sour cream, mayonnaise and green onion tops in a food processor. Process until mixed. Serve with fresh vegetables or chips.

Yield: 6 servings

*Make a beautiful dinner for your favorite Valentine.
It will be a treat for both of you!*

Light Caesar Salad

1/2 **red onion, thinly sliced**
2 **bags romaine lettuce**
6 **tablespoons light Caesar salad dressing**
2 **tablespoons (6 teaspoons) grated Parmesan cheese**

Arrange the onion slices over the lettuce on salad plates. Drizzle 1 tablespoon of the salad dressing over each salad. Sprinkle each with 1 teaspoon of the cheese.

Yield: 6 servings

For added flavor, try topping this salad with garlic-flavored croutons.

Crawfish Nita

1 cup (2 sticks) butter (not margarine)
1 cup chopped green onions
16 ounces hot Mexican Velveeta cheese, cubed
1/2 cup white wine
2 pounds frozen crawfish tails, thawed

Melt the butter in a skillet. Add the green onions and sauté briefly. Add the cheese. Cook until the cheese melts, stirring constantly. Stir in the wine and crawfish tails. Cook until heated through. Serve over cooked bow tie or shell pasta.

Yield: 8 servings

This recipe is a "Test Kitchen" favorite. It is even better the second day. (It freezes well, too.)

Adrienne's Chocolate Pie

2 (4-ounce) packages chocolate instant pudding mix
3 1/2 cups cold milk
8 ounces whipped topping
1 (9-inch) graham cracker pie shell
2 cups sliced strawberries

Combine the pudding mix and cold milk in a mixing bowl and beat for 1 minute. Fold in half the whipped topping. Spoon into the pie shell. Chill for 1 hour. Top each serving with some of the remaining whipped topping and the sliced strawberries.

Yield: 8 servings

- - - -

When it's cold outside, set up tables and chairs in front of the fireplace. Your family will love having supper in front of a warm fire.

Four Carb Cheesecake

32 ounces cream cheese, softened
1 cup aspartame sweetener
4 eggs
2 teaspoons vanilla extract
1 pint fresh strawberries, sliced

Spray a 9-inch springform pan with nonstick cooking spray. Beat the cream cheese in a mixing bowl until smooth. Beat in the sweetener gradually. Add the eggs 1 at a time, beating well after each addition. Beat in the vanilla. Spoon into the prepared pan. Bake at 350 degrees for 15 minutes. Reduce the oven temperature to 275 degrees. Bake for 1 hour. Turn off the oven. Let stand in the closed oven for 2 hours. Chill until serving time. Top with the strawberries.

Yield: 12 servings

This sugar-free cheesecake is big on flavor. Try topping it off with blueberries or other favorite berries.

Chance Cheesy Soup

1 (16-ounce) package frozen Cheddar Pasta Accents
2 (10-ounce) cans cream of celery soup
3 cups milk
1 teaspoon seasoning salt
1 cup (4 ounces) shredded Cheddar cheese with jalapeño chiles

Cook the pasta using the package directions; drain.
Combine the pasta, undiluted soup, milk and seasoning salt in
a large saucepan and mix well. Stir in the cheese. Cook until
heated through, stirring occasionally.

Yield: 6 servings

----

*Pasta and cheese make this homemade
soup good enough for company. (It's also ready
in less than an hour.)*

Mom's Chicken Soup

2 boneless skinless chicken breasts, cut into bite-size pieces
5 cups chicken broth
1 (10-ounce) package frozen mixed onions, bell peppers and celery
1 (10-ounce) package frozen peas
1 cup uncooked seashell pasta (conchiglie)

Combine the chicken, chicken broth and frozen vegetables in a medium saucepan. Simmer, covered, until the vegetables are tender, stirring occasionally. Stir in the peas and pasta. Cook for 15 minutes or until the pasta is tender and the chicken is cooked through.

Yield: 6 servings

▬ ▬ ▬ ▬

For a baby shower, choose a toy (such as a plastic truck or small colorful wagon) to hold the floral centerpiece. After the party, the guest of honor can take the toy home.

Christopher's Black Bean Soup

3 (15-ounce) cans black beans

1/2 cup chopped carrots

1 (10-ounce) package frozen mixed onions, bell peppers and celery

1 cup cubed cooked ham

1 (10-ounce) can tomatoes with green chiles

Combine the undrained beans, carrots, frozen vegetables, ham and tomatoes with chiles in a medium stockpot. Cook until bubbly and heated through, stirring occasionally.

Yield: 8 servings

- - - -

A soup and salad supper is a great way to have a family gathering while watching your favorite football team. A coffee table can become a buffet to hold extra drinks and desserts.

Black Beans and Rice

1 envelope dry onion soup mix
1 pound beef link sausage, cut into small pieces
3 (15-ounce) cans black beans
1 (10-ounce) can tomatoes with green chiles
1 large green bell pepper, chopped

Combine the dry soup mix, sausage, undrained black beans, undrained tomatoes with chiles and bell pepper in a large Dutch oven or slow cooker. Cook over low to medium heat for 2 hours or longer, adding water if needed. Serve over hot cooked rice.

Yield: 6 servings

■ ▬ ■ ▬ ■

Try topping this dish with sour cream and shredded Cheddar cheese.

Pasta Kimbriel

1 cup sliced yellow squash
1 cup sliced zucchini
2 tablespoons olive oil
1 (16-ounce) jar sun-dried tomato Alfredo sauce
2 cups linguini, cooked and drained

Sauté the squash and zucchini in the olive oil in a saucepan. Add the Alfredo sauce and mix well. Cook until heated through, stirring occasionally. Serve over the linguini.

Yield: 4 servings

Serve this wonderful pasta with a simple packaged salad and a loaf of deli French bread.

Take 5... Menus of Spring

St. Paddy's Day Gathering

- - - -

March Madness Chili Supper

- - - -

Easy Easter Lunch

Mother's Day Dinner

- - - -

Spring Fever Luncheon

- - - -

Family Reunion Picnic

- - - -

Fast-Lane Dinners for Spring

Lemonade Tea Punch

10 cups water
2 family-size decaffeinated tea bags
1 cup sugar
1 (6-ounce) can frozen lemonade concentrate

Bring the water to a boil in a large saucepan. Add the tea bags. Remove from the heat and steep, covered, for 15 minutes. Remove and discard the tea bags. Add the sugar and lemonade concentrate to the tea and mix well. Chill until serving time.

Yield: 10 servings

This punch is a great way to start a large meal. It can also be served in small glass cups for a special occasion.

Shrimp Dip Stroble

8 ounces cream cheese, softened
1 (3-ounce) jar cocktail sauce
1 (4-ounce) can shrimp, drained and chopped
1 cup (4 ounces) shredded Monterey Jack cheese with jalapeños
4 green onions, chopped

Spread the cream cheese on a large plate. Cover with the cocktail sauce. Layer the shrimp, Monterey Jack cheese and green onions over the cocktail sauce. Chill for 30 minutes. Serve with corn chips.

Yield: 12 servings

Decorating the napkins is a great way for kids to help during the holidays. Raffia and ribbon are easy to tie around a napkin. Even the plainest napkin can be dressed up with a plaid ribbon.

Beef Pot Roast

1 (3-pound) beef roast
1 (10-ounce) can cream of mushroom soup
1 envelope dried onion soup mix

Place the roast in a baking pan. Cover with the undiluted mushroom soup and sprinkle with the dry soup mix. Bake, covered with foil, at 300 degrees for 3 hours. This roast makes its own gravy.

Yield: 6 servings

- - - -

Make this one-dish meal and tuck half of it in the freezer. Pull it out during the busy holiday season, so you will have time to shop till you drop.

Twice-Baked Potatoes

8 medium baking potatoes, baked
2 tablespoons butter
1 (10-ounce) can Cheddar cheese soup
1 tablespoon chopped dried chives
1 cup (4 ounces) shredded sharp Cheddar cheese

Cut each potato in half lengthwise. Scoop out the pulp,
leaving a thin shell. Combine the potato pulp and butter in a mixing
bowl. Beat until blended. Add the undiluted soup, chives and cheese
and mix well. Spoon into the potato shells. Place the potato shells in a
large baking dish. Bake at 450 degrees for 15 minutes.

Yield: 8 servings

---

*Fresh herbs may be used instead of dried
in most recipes in a ratio of 3:1, that is, three units of
fresh herbs equal one unit of dried herbs.*

Marinated Green Beans

4 (15-ounce) cans green beans, drained
2 (14-ounce) cans artichoke hearts, drained
1$\frac{1}{2}$ cups sugar
1 cup olive oil
1 (8-ounce) bottle oil and vinegar salad dressing

Combine the green beans and artichoke hearts in a large bowl. Heat the sugar, olive oil and salad dressing in a small saucepan until the sugar is dissolved, stirring constantly. Pour over the green bean mixture and stir to coat. Chill, covered, overnight.

Yield: 12 servings

■ ■ ■ ■

Keep the salt in your salt shaker from clumping together by adding a few grains of rice to the salt.

Corn Soufflé

1 (16-ounce) package frozen corn kernels, thawed
5 eggs, lightly beaten
1^1/$_2$ cups half-and-half
^{1}/$_4$ cup (^{1}/$_2$ stick) butter, melted
^{1}/$_4$ cup chopped onion

Combine the corn, eggs, half-and-half, butter and onion
in a bowl and mix well. Spoon into a lightly greased baking dish.
Bake at 350 degrees for 1 hour.

Yield: 8 servings

_A tailgate or picnic is a great way to use old
plaid tablecloths and napkins. Place fresh
flowers in a large Mason jar, and use small jars to
hold spoons, knives, and forks._

Aunt Jan's Apple Pie

1 cup packed brown sugar
1/2 cup half-and-half
1/2 cup (1 stick) butter or margarine
1/2 cup chopped pecans, toasted
1 frozen apple pie, baked

Combine the brown sugar, half-and-half and butter in a small saucepan. Bring to a boil over medium heat. Cook for 1 minute, stirring constantly. Remove from the heat and stir in the pecans. Cool slightly. Spoon the warm sauce over slices of pie.

Yield: 8 servings

■ ■ — ■

The praline topping will make this frozen pie take center stage. Only Aunt Jan knows our secret.

Hearty Rotel Dip

1 pound hot sausage
1 pound ground beef
2 pounds Velveeta cheese, cut into pieces
1 (10-ounce) can cream of mushroom soup
1 (10-ounce) can Rotel tomatoes (tomatoes with green chiles)

Brown the sausage and ground beef in a skillet, stirring until crumbly; drain well. Combine with the cheese, undiluted soup and tomatoes with chiles in a bowl and mix well. Spoon into a baking dish. Bake at 350 degrees for 20 minutes or until bubbly and heated through. Serve with corn chip scoops.

Yield: 10 servings

- - - -

For Ranch Potato Skins, cut 4 baked potatoes into quarters and scoop out the pulp, leaving a thin shell. Mix the pulp with 1/4 cup sour cream and 1 envelope ranch salad dressing mix and spoon into the potato shells. Sprinkle each with about 1 1/4 tablespoons Cheddar cheese. Bake at 375 degrees for 12 to 15 minutes.

Black Bean Chili

1 pound ground beef or ground turkey
1 envelope chili seasoning mix
2 (8-ounce) cans tomato sauce
2 (15-ounce) cans black beans
1 (14-ounce) can chicken broth

Brown the ground beef in a skillet, stirring until crumbly;
drain well. Add the seasoning mix, tomato sauce, beans and
chicken broth and mix well. Simmer, covered,
for 1 hour, stirring frequently.

Yield: 6 servings

This chili is great with corn bread or corn muffins.

Crunchy Coleslaw

1 (3-ounce) package beef-flavored ramen noodles
2 tablespoons sugar
1 (16-ounce) bag shredded coleslaw mix
1 (5-ounce) package sliced almonds
1/2 cup bottled vinegar and oil salad dressing

Mix the contents of the noodle seasoning packet and the sugar in a large bowl. Crush the noodles and add to the sugar mixture. Add the coleslaw mix and almonds and mix well. Drizzle with the salad dressing and toss to coat. Chill, covered, until serving time.

Yield: 8 servings

- - - -

Food should be the focal point of a plate, so keep the entire border or rim of the plate empty.

Southern Corn Bread

3 cups self-rising cornmeal
2$^{1}/_{4}$ cups buttermilk
$^{1}/_{3}$ cup vegetable oil
2 eggs, beaten

Combine the cornmeal, buttermilk, oil and eggs in a
bowl and mix well. Pour into a greased ovenproof skillet. Bake
at 425 degrees for 25 minutes.

Yield: 12 servings

■ ■ ■ ■

*This recipe works well in muffin cups, too.
Grease the muffin cups or spray them with
nonstick cooking spray.*

Speedy Peanut Butter Pie

1 cup chunky peanut butter
1 cup sugar
8 ounces cream cheese, softened
1/2 cup milk
12 ounces whipped topping

Combine the peanut butter, sugar, cream cheese, milk and whipped topping in a mixing bowl and mix well. Spoon into two 9-inch chocolate crumb pie shells. Freeze until serving time.

Yield: 12 servings

- - - -

Entertain a large group of friends the easy way—with a dessert party. (Forget counting calories or fat grams for the day!) Serve simple desserts on a buffet and enjoy watching everyone have fun.

Hot Fudge Sauce

1/4 cup (1/2 stick) butter or margarine
1 cup (6 ounces) chocolate chips
1 cup heavy cream
1 cup confectioners' sugar
1 teaspoon vanilla extract

Combine the butter, chocolate chips and cream in a microwave-safe bowl. Microwave on Medium for 1-minute intervals until the butter and chocolate chips are melted and smooth, stirring after each interval. Stir in the confectioners' sugar. Microwave on High for 6 minutes, stirring 3 times. Stir in the vanilla. Store, covered, in the refrigerator. Heat before each use. Serve over ice cream or Almost Effortless Ice Cream Pie (page 120).

Yield: 2 cups

If you want to serve coffee with dessert, brew the coffee before the guests arrive and keep it hot in a thermos.

Southern Iced Tea

1¹/₂ quarts water
2 small tea bags
1 cup sugar
2 tablespoons lemon juice

Bring the water to a boil in a saucepan. Remove from the heat and add the tea bags. Let steep for 2 to 4 hours or until lukewarm. Stir in the sugar and lemon juice. Pour into a pitcher and chill thoroughly. Serve very cold over ice.

Yield: 6 servings

Did you know that it isn't necessary for all your china to match? You can use different patterns as long as they coordinate. Be creative!

Ginger's English Muffins

1 1/2 cups (6 ounces) shredded sharp Cheddar cheese
1 cup chopped green onions
1 cup chopped black olives
1/2 cup mayonnaise
6 English muffins, split into halves

Combine the cheese, green onions, olives and mayonnaise
in a bowl and mix well. Spread on the cut side of the muffin halves.
Place on a baking sheet. Bake at 350 degrees for 20 to 25 minutes or
until the cheese is melted. Cut into triangles.

Yield: 24 servings

Use small pots of red geraniums to add color to your dinner table. They will bloom for weeks.

Tina's Fruit Delight

3 (15-ounce) cans chunky mixed fruit, drained
1 (4-ounce) jar maraschino cherries, drained
1 cup pecans, chopped
1/2 cup (1 stick) butter, melted
3/4 cup packed brown sugar

Combine the mixed fruit, maraschino cherries and pecans
in a 9×13-inch baking dish. Mix the butter and brown sugar in a
bowl. Pour over the fruit mixture. Bake at 325 degrees for 1 hour.

Yield: 10 servings

▬ ▬ ▬ ▬

Substitute fresh fruit in season in this recipe.

Deviled Eggs

6 eggs, hard-cooked and peeled
2 tablespoons mayonnaise
1 tablespoon sweet pickle relish
1 teaspoon prepared mustard
1/8 teaspoon salt

Cut the eggs into halves lengthwise. Mash the egg yolks in a bowl. Add the mayonnaise, relish, prepared mustard and salt and mix well. Spoon into the egg whites. Garnish with paprika. Place the eggs on a serving plate and chill until serving time.

Yield: 6 servings

▬ ▬ ▬ ▬

Easter would not be complete without these stuffed eggs on the table. Peel hard-cooked eggs under cold water for easier removal of the shells.

Kristen's Poppy Seed Chicken

10 chicken breasts

3 cups sour cream

2 (10-ounce) cans cream of chicken soup

1/4 cup poppy seeds

1 cup crushed butter crackers

Remove and discard the chicken skin and bones. Arrange the chicken in a single layer in a 9×13-inch baking dish. Mix the sour cream, undiluted soup and poppy seeds in a bowl. Spoon over the chicken. Top with the cracker crumbs. Bake at 350 degrees for 1 hour or until the chicken is cooked through.

Yield: 6 servings

To keep your meal hot, rinse plates with very hot tap water before serving the food. Dry the plates and fill them with hot food.

Spinach Cheese Casserole

2 (10-ounce) packages frozen chopped spinach
1 (10-ounce) can cream of mushroom soup
2 eggs, beaten
1 cup mayonnaise
1 cup (4 ounces) shredded sharp Cheddar cheese

Cook the spinach using the package directions; drain well. Combine the spinach, undiluted soup, eggs, mayonnaise and cheese in a bowl and mix well. Spoon into a 9×13-inch baking dish. Bake at 350 degrees for 45 minutes.

Yield: 12 servings

■ ■ ■

An easy, quick side dish . . . hearty enough for a steak supper.

Blue Ribbon Bread

2 envelopes dry yeast
2 cups warm water (105 to 115 degrees)
5 cups baking mix (not low-fat)
1/4 cup sugar
4 eggs, beaten

Sprinkle the yeast over the water in a large bowl. Stir until the yeast dissolves. Stir in the baking mix, sugar and eggs. Let rise, covered, in a warm place for 1 1/2 hours or until doubled in bulk. Punch down the dough and divide into 2 equal portions. Shape each portion into a loaf and place in a greased loaf pan. Let rise for 1 hour. Bake at 350 degrees for 35 minutes.

Yield: 2 loaves

- - - -

A new twist on an old favorite, this is a great bread to team up with your holiday meal.

Patsy's Lemon Cream Cake

1 (2-layer) package pudding-recipe lemon cake mix
2 (14-ounce) cans sweetened condensed milk
2/3 cup lemon juice
8 ounces whipped topping

Prepare and bake the cake mix using the package directions for two 8-inch cake pans. Cool as directed. Mix half the condensed milk and half the lemon juice in a bowl. Spread between the cake layers. Mix the remaining condensed milk, remaining lemon juice and the whipped topping in a bowl. Spread over the top and side of the cake. Chill until serving time.

Yield: 12 servings

This cake is a dream, and it's even better the second day.

Summer Salad

1 (8-ounce) can English peas, drained
1 cup (4 ounces) shredded mild Cheddar cheese
1/2 cup finely chopped onion
1 cup minced dill pickles
1/2 cup mayonnaise

Combine the English peas, cheese, onion, pickles and mayonnaise in a bowl and mix well. Chill, covered, until serving time.

Yield: 4 to 6 servings

- - - - -

If you are on a budget, buy napkins and paper plates at the end of each season. By year's end, you will be ready for all occasions.

Pat's Chicken Eden Isle

6 chicken breasts

Pepper to taste

2 (10-ounce) cans cream of chicken soup

1 cup sour cream

8 ounces cream cheese, softened

Remove and discard the chicken skin and bones. Sprinkle the chicken with pepper. Arrange the chicken in a single layer in a 9×13-inch baking dish. Combine the undiluted soup, sour cream and cream cheese in a bowl and mix well. Spoon over the chicken. Bake, covered tightly with foil, at 300 degrees for 2 hours or until tender. Remove the foil and let the top brown. Serve over rice or noodles.

Yield: 6 servings

■ ■ ▪ ■

To soften cream cheese or butter, unwrap it and microwave on High for 30 seconds.

Southern Fried Beans

4 slices bacon, diced
1 small onion, chopped
1/2 cup water
1 tablespoon sugar
2 (15-ounce) cans yellow wax beans, drained

Cook the bacon and onion in a skillet until the bacon is crisp, stirring frequently; drain well. Combine the bacon mixture, water, sugar and beans in the skillet and mix well. Cook, covered, for 20 minutes.

Yield: 6 servings

- - - -

When purchasing pre-bagged produce, such as apples or potatoes, weigh several bags to find the heaviest. They can sometimes vary by as much as a pound.

Fresh Mushroom Casserole

1/2 cup (1 stick) butter
3 (8-ounce) packages sliced fresh mushrooms
1 1/2 cups herb-seasoned stuffing mix
2 cups (8 ounces) shredded sharp Cheddar cheese
1/2 cup half-and-half

Melt the butter in a skillet. Add the mushrooms and sauté
until tender. Stir in the stuffing mix. Spoon into a 9×13-inch baking dish.
Top with the cheese. Pour the half-and-half over the top. Bake
at 350 degrees for 20 minutes.

Yield: 6 servings

■ ■ ■ ■

*The word "sauté" means to cook food quickly
in a small amount of oil or butter.*

No-Fail Bread

1 envelope dry yeast
1 tablespoon sugar
$1/2$ cup warm water
4 cups self-rising flour
$1^1/_2$ cups water

Dissolve the yeast and sugar in the warm water in a bowl. Add the flour and $1^1/_2$ cups water gradually, mixing after each addition. Knead on a floured surface until smooth and elastic. Place in a greased bowl, turning to coat the dough. Let rise, covered, in a warm place until doubled in bulk. Punch down dough. Divide into 2 equal portions. Shape each portion into a loaf. Place in a loaf pan sprayed with nonstick cooking spray. Bake at 375 degrees for 35 minutes or until brown.

Yield: 2 loaves

— — — —

To activate yeast, the liquid in which it is placed must be between 105 and 115 degrees. Use a candy thermometer, and your bread will never fail.

Beth's Good Pies

1 cup chopped pecans or walnuts
1 (14-ounce) can sweetened condensed milk
8 ounces cream cheese, softened
8 ounces whipped topping
2 (9-inch) graham cracker pie shells

Combine the pecans, condensed milk, cream cheese and whipped topping in a bowl and mix well. Spoon into the pie shells. Freeze until serving time. Top with purchased caramel sauce.

Yield: 12 servings

- - - -

Many stores carry shelled fresh nuts in the produce section.

Best Party Punch

2 (6-ounce) cans frozen lemonade concentrate, thawed
2 (6-ounce) cans frozen orange juice concentrate, thawed
2 (6-ounce) cans frozen limeade concentrate, thawed
8 cups cold water
2 quarts ginger ale, chilled

Combine all the concentrates with the cold water in a large container and mix well. Pour over ice in a punch bowl. Stir in the ginger ale just before serving.

Yield: 25 servings

■ ■ ■ ■

To make an ice ring for a punch bowl, reserve 4 cups of the punch and pour it into a round gelatin mold. Stir in a jar of maraschino cherries (without the stems) and freeze for 8 hours.

Mississippi Sin

1 baguette French bread
1 (8-ounce) container French onion dip
2 cups (8 ounces) shredded sharp Cheddar cheese
8 ounces cream cheese, softened
1 (4-ounce) can chopped green chiles, drained

Cut the top off the bread and reserve. Scoop out the bread from the center of the loaf; discard or reserve for use as bread crumbs. Mix the onion dip, Cheddar cheese, cream cheese and green chiles in a bowl. Spoon into the hollowed-out bread loaf and replace the top. Wrap in foil and place on a baking sheet. Bake at 350 degrees for 1 hour. Remove the top of the bread. Serve with corn chips.

Yield: 8 servings

- - - -

Mark the recipes you use most often with a paper clip or sticky note.

Tricia's Tortellini Salad

1 (9-ounce) package refrigerator 3-cheese tortellini
1 (10-ounce) can chopped chicken breast, drained
1/2 cup ranch salad dressing
1 Granny Smith apple, chopped
Tops only of 4 green onions, chopped

Cook the tortellini using the package directions; drain. Combine the tortellini, chicken, salad dressing, apple and green onions in a bowl and mix well. Cover and chill. Serve on a bed of fresh spinach or other salad greens.

Yield: 6 servings

- - - -

This salad makes a perfect lunch or light dinner entrée. Garnish it with chopped walnuts or sliced almonds.

Parmesan Spinach

2 (10-ounce) packages frozen chopped spinach,
thawed and drained
1 egg, beaten
1 cup cottage cheese
1 cup (4 ounces) grated Parmesan cheese
2 tablespoons butter, melted

Combine the spinach, egg, cottage cheese, Parmesan cheese
and butter in a bowl and mix well. Spoon into a baking dish. Bake at
350 degrees for 30 minutes or until heated through.

Yield: 8 servings

- - - -

*To avoid foods splattering in the microwave,
use a round bowl and cover with a heatproof
round casserole cover.*

Piña Colada Fruit Dip

12 ounces cream cheese, softened

3/4 cup piña colada mix

1/2 cup sour cream

1 1/4 cups crushed pineapple

1/2 cup maraschino cherries, sliced

Combine the cream cheese, piña colada mix, sour cream, pineapple and maraschino cherries in a bowl and mix well. Chill, covered, for 1 hour. Serve with fresh fruit in season.

Yield: 8 servings

For easier pouring of sticky items like honey, spray measuring cups and pitchers with nonstick cooking spray before measuring.

Best Biscuits

2 cups baking mix
1 cup heavy cream
Butter

Combine the baking mix and cream in a bowl and mix well.
Pat the dough 3/4 inch thick on a floured surface. Cut with a biscuit
cutter. Place on a baking sheet. Bake at 400 degrees for
12 minutes or until golden brown. Serve with butter.

Yield: About 1 dozen

- - - -

Try to gather your family around the table for meals as often as possible. The table is the one place families can all share a positive time together.

No-Cook Angel Cake

1 (14-ounce) deli angel food cake
1 cup confectioners' sugar
8 ounces cream cheese, softened
8 ounces whipped topping
2 (21-ounce) cans blueberry pie filling

Cut the cake into 1-inch cubes. Cream the confectioners'
sugar and cream cheese in a mixing bowl until light and fluffy.
Fold in the whipped topping and cake cubes. Spread evenly in a
9×13-inch dish. Top with the pie filling. Chill, covered, for 2 hours or
longer. Cut into squares to serve.

Yield: 12 to 15 servings

*Make this cake and invite friends over for
dessert and coffee. Keep sugar-free ice cream in
your freezer in case one of your guests is on
a special diet.*

Tortilla Roll-Ups

8 ounces cream cheese, softened
1 (4-ounce) can chopped green chiles, drained
1 (2-ounce) can chopped black olives, drained
10 large flour tortillas
1 (16-ounce) jar salsa

Combine the cream cheese, green chiles and olives in
a bowl and mix well. Spread over the tortillas; roll up to enclose the
filling. Chill, covered, overnight. Cut the tortillas into 1/2-inch slices.
Serve with the salsa.

Yield: 20 servings

■ ■ ■

*These quick rolls are easy to prepare and
perfect for any holiday meal.*

Sarah's Black Cherry Salad

2 (3-ounce) packages black cherry gelatin
2 cups boiling water
1 (15-ounce) can Bing cherries in heavy syrup
1 (20-ounce) can pineapple chunks or tidbits
1 cup chopped pecans

Combine the gelatin and boiling water in a bowl, stirring until the gelatin is dissolved. Drain the cherries and pineapple, reserving the juice. Pour the juice into a measuring cup. Add enough water to measure 2 cups liquid. Stir into the gelatin. Add the cherries, pineapple and pecans and mix well. Chill, covered, until set.

Yield: 8 servings

Use colorful bandanas to line your bread baskets for a backyard barbecue. The bandanas can double as dinner napkins.

Slow Cooker Brisket

1 (3- to 3^1/$_2$-pound) brisket, cut into halves
1 cup ketchup
^{1}/$_4$ cup apple jelly
1 envelope onion soup mix
^{1}/$_2$ teaspoon pepper

Place 1 piece of the brisket in a slow cooker. Mix the ketchup, jelly, dry soup mix and pepper in a bowl. Spread half the mixture over the brisket. Top with the remaining brisket and spread with the remaining ketchup mixture. Cook, covered, on Low for 8 to 10 hours or until the brisket is tender. Cut into slices. Serve with the cooking juices.

Yield: 8 to 10 servings

- - - - -

In addition to allowing you to make soups while you're away from home, a slow cooker lets you buy inexpensive cuts of meat and turn them into delicious meals for your family.

Mexican Corn Casserole

1/2 cup (1 stick) butter
1 onion, chopped
2 (8-ounce) cans Mexican-style corn, drained
2 cups cooked white rice
1 (10-ounce) can cream of mushroom soup

Melt the butter in a skillet. Add the onion and sauté until tender. Add the corn, rice and undiluted soup and mix well. Pour into a greased baking dish. Bake at 350 degrees for 30 minutes.

Yield: 6 to 8 servings

- - - -

Peel vegetables directly over the garbage disposal for easier cleanup.

Tangy Potato Salad

4 or 5 potatoes
2 tablespoons prepared mustard
2 tablespoons mayonnaise
1 small onion, chopped
1 (2-ounce) jar pimento, drained

Boil the potatoes in water to cover in a saucepan; drain.
Peel and dice the potatoes. Combine the potatoes, prepared
mustard, mayonnaise, onion and pimento in a bowl and
mix well. Chill, covered, until serving time.

Yield: 6 to 8 servings

- - - -

*Use empty small glass soda bottles to hold
flowers for an easy summer tablescape.
Wildflowers will work.*

Sour Cream Pound Cake

1 (2-layer) package butter-recipe yellow cake mix
1 cup (2 sticks) margarine, melted
1 cup sour cream
4 eggs, beaten
1 teaspoon vanilla extract

Combine the cake mix, margarine, sour cream, eggs and vanilla in a bowl and mix well. Pour into a greased tube pan. Bake at 325 degrees for 1 hour. Cool in the pan. Invert onto a serving plate.

Yield: 12 servings

This easy-to-make dessert will remind you of Sunday lunch at your grandmama's house.

Cashew Chicken Salad

6 chicken breasts, cooked and chopped
1 (8-ounce) can pineapple chunks, drained
1 cup mayonnaise
1 teaspoon curry powder
1 cup cashews

Mix the chicken, pineapple, mayonnaise and curry powder in a bowl. Cover and chill. Stir in the cashews just before serving.

Yield: 6 servings

- - - -

Prepare Grilled Tuna Steaks by brushing four fresh tuna steaks with a mixture of 1/2 cup olive oil, 1/4 cup lemon juice, and 1 teaspoon each salt and pepper. Grill for 2 to 3 minutes per side for medium rare.

Pearl's Chicken Pie

1 (5-ounce) can evaporated milk
1 (10-ounce) can cream of chicken soup
1 (3-ounce) can chicken, drained
1 (15-ounce) can mixed vegetables, drained
2 refrigerator pie pastries

Combine the evaporated milk, undiluted soup, chicken and mixed vegetables in a bowl and mix well. Spoon into a 9×13-inch baking dish. Unfold the pie pastries and place over the baking dish, overlapping slightly. Trim away any excess pastry. Bake at 350 degrees for 45 minutes.

Yield: 6 servings

You can use leftover turkey in this dish. Your family will never know.

Chicken Burritos

4 boneless skinless chicken breasts, chopped
1 (16-ounce) jar medium salsa
2 cups (8 ounces) shredded Cheddar cheese
1 1/2 cups sour cream
6 (10-inch) flour tortillas

Combine the chicken and half the salsa in a skillet. Cook for 4 to 5 minutes or until the chicken is cooked through, stirring frequently. Add 1 1/2 cups of the cheese and the sour cream and mix well. Spoon onto the tortillas and fold to enclose the filling. Place seam side down in a baking dish. Top with the remaining salsa and cheese. Bake at 350 degrees for 20 to 25 minutes or until heated through.

Yield: 6 servings

- - - -

Use an ice cream scoop to evenly divide chicken salad, muffins, or cupcake batter.

Mexican Chicken

1 envelope taco seasoning mix
1 pound boneless chicken breasts, cut into strips
1 tablespoon vegetable oil
1 (14-ounce) can diced tomatoes
1/2 cup peach preserves

Spread the seasoning mix on a plate. Roll the chicken strips in the seasoning mix until coated. Heat the oil in a large skillet over medium heat. Add the chicken. Sauté for 5 to 7 minutes or until cooked through. Stir in the tomatoes and preserves. Simmer, covered, for 10 minutes.

Yield: 4 servings

▬ ▬ ▬ ▬

Serve your meal buffet style: Offering food from a sideboard or a buffet allows more room on the table for a centerpiece or creative place cards.

Take 5... Menus of Summer

Father's Day: "Fire Up the Grill"

- - - -

Fourth of July Celebration

- - - -

A Poolside Dinner

Informal Dessert Buffet

- - - -

Labor Day Cookout

- - - -

End-of-Summer Supper

- - - -

Fast-Lane Dinners for Summer

Cheesy Broccoli Dip

2 cups (8 ounces) shredded sharp Cheddar cheese
8 ounces cream cheese, softened
1 cup sour cream
1 (10-ounce) package frozen chopped broccoli,
thawed and drained
1 teaspoon salt

Combine the Cheddar cheese, cream cheese, sour cream,
broccoli and salt in a bowl and mix well. Spoon into a baking dish.
Bake at 350 degrees for 25 minutes. Serve with chips.

Yield: 12 servings

- - - -

*If you do not have a large metal tub in which to ice
down your drinks, line a big basket with a thick black
plastic bag. Fill it with ice and enjoy!*

Grilled Portobello Salad

1/2 cup extra-virgin olive oil

1/3 cup balsamic vinegar

2 garlic cloves, minced

Juice of 1 lemon

4 large portobello mushrooms

Combine the olive oil, vinegar, garlic and lemon juice in a shallow dish. Add the mushrooms and marinate for 10 to 15 minutes. Drain well, discarding the marinade. Grill the mushrooms for 3 to 4 minutes per side. Serve over a bed of fresh spinach.

Yield: 4 servings

- - - -

Quick, easy, and heart healthy.

Always Sunday Steaks

1 (8-ounce) bottle Italian salad dressing
1/2 cup Worcestershire sauce
Juice of 1 lemon
1/2 cup steak sauce
4 rib-eye steaks

Combine the salad dressing, Worcestershire sauce, lemon juice and steak sauce in a sealable plastic bag. Add the steaks and seal the bag. Marinate in the refrigerator for 2 hours. Drain well, discarding the marinade. Grill over moderate heat to desired degree of doneness.

Yield: 4 servings

This versatile marinade works well for beef, pork, or chicken.

Grilled Vegetable Kabobs

Fresh vegetables
1 cup bottled Italian salad dressing

Cut fresh vegetables into large chunks (enough to make about 4 cups). Combine the salad dressing and vegetables in a large bowl and toss gently to mix. Marinate for 1 hour. Drain well, discarding the marinade. Thread the vegetables onto skewers. Grill over hot coals for 10 minutes. Vegetables such as squash, cherry tomatoes, whole mushrooms and zucchini work well in this recipe.

Yield: 4 servings

- - - -

To decorate your table for a summer luncheon, use old colorful cups or bowls. Fill several with zinnias or roses from the yard. (If you don't grow flowers, buy a package of fresh daisies to fill the cups.)

Robert's House Potatoes

4 cups (about) dried potato flakes
8 ounces cream cheese, softened
1 (8-ounce) container French onion dip
2 cups (8 ounces) shredded sharp Cheddar cheese
1 (6-ounce) can French-fried onions

Prepare the mashed potatoes using the package directions.
Stir in the cream cheese and onion dip. Spoon into a greased
9×13-inch baking dish. Cover with the Cheddar cheese. Top with
the onions. Bake at 300 degrees for 30 minutes.

Yield: 6 servings

▬ ▬ ▬ ▬

*Your family will love every bite of these "dressed up"
mashed potatoes!*

Peach Cobbler

1/4 cup (1/2 stick) butter, melted
3/4 cup self-rising flour
1/2 cup sugar
1/2 cup milk
2 cups sliced peaches

Spread the butter in a baking dish. Mix the flour, sugar and milk in a bowl and pour into the baking dish. Spoon the peaches over the flour mixture. Bake at 350 degrees for 1 hour.

Yield: 6 servings

- - - -

Fresh peaches are one of the favorite fruits of summer, and there's no better way to enjoy peaches than in a cobbler.

Family-Size Broccoli

1 (16-ounce) package frozen chopped broccoli
2 packages chicken-flavored rice and vermicelli
2 (10-ounce) cans cream of chicken soup
16 ounces Velveeta or American cheese, cut into cubes
1/2 teaspoon cayenne pepper

Cook the broccoli using the package directions; drain.
Cook the rice using the package directions. Combine the
broccoli, rice, undiluted soup, cheese and cayenne pepper in
a bowl and mix well. Spoon into two 9×13-inch baking dishes.
Bake at 350 degrees for 20 minutes.

Yield: 16 servings

---

*You can always have fresh lemon juice if you
buy whole lemons on sale and freeze them. Thaw
them in the microwave before juicing.*

Brenda's Red Grape Salad

8 ounces cream cheese, softened
1 cup sour cream
2 pounds red seedless grapes
1 cup packed dark brown sugar
1 cup chopped pecans

Mix the cream cheese and sour cream in a bowl. Fold in the grapes. Spoon into a 9×13-inch glass dish. Top with the brown sugar and pecans. Chill, covered, for 1 hour.

Yield: 8 servings

- - - -

Never pass up a good sale. Buy red glass or paper plates after Christmas and use them for Valentine's Day, the Fourth of July, or an end of summer picnic.

Best-Ever Burgers

2 pounds ground beef
1 envelope onion soup mix
1/2 cup water
8 hamburger buns

Combine the ground beef, soup mix and water in a bowl and mix well. Shape into 8 patties. Grill over medium heat until cooked through. Serve on the buns.

Yield: 8 servings

- - - -

For El Rancho Potato Salad, combine 16 cooked and sliced unpeeled red potatoes, 1 cup bacon bits, 1 cup chopped green olives, 8 chopped green onions, and 2 cups ranch salad dressing in a large bowl and mix well. Chill, covered, until serving time. Yield: 8 servings.

Oven-Baked Beans

1/2 pound ground beef
1 small onion, chopped
2 (16-ounce) cans pork and beans
1/2 cup barbecue sauce
1/2 cup packed brown sugar

Brown the ground beef with the onion in an ovenproof skillet, stirring until the ground beef is crumbly; drain well. Combine the ground beef mixture, pork and beans, barbecue sauce and brown sugar in the skillet and mix well. Bake at 350 degrees for 1 hour. These beans can be cooked in a slow cooker on High for 3 hours instead of in the oven.

Yield: 10 servings

Grilled meat and a potluck of fresh salads make a simple supper on a warm summer night.

American Berry Cheesecake

16 ounces cream cheese, softened
1/3 cup sugar
8 ounces whipped topping
1 (9-inch) graham cracker pie shell
Strawberry halves and blueberries

Beat the cream cheese and sugar at medium speed in a mixer bowl until blended. Fold in 2 cups of the whipped topping. Spoon into the pie shell. Chill for 3 hours or until set. Spread the remaining whipped topping over the top. Top with strawberries and blueberries.

Yield: 12 servings

- - - -

Arrange the strawberries and blueberries in rows to resemble the American flag.

Barbara's Asparagus Roll-Ups

10 large flour tortillas
8 ounces cream cheese, softened
2 teaspoons seasoned salt
2 (14-ounce) cans asparagus spears, drained
1/2 cup (2 ounces) grated fresh Parmesan cheese

Cut the tortillas into quarters. Mix the cream cheese and seasoned salt in a bowl. Spread over the tortilla pieces. Place 1 piece of asparagus on each piece and roll up. Arrange the rolls in a single layer in 2 greased 9×13-inch baking dishes. Sprinkle with the Parmesan cheese. Bake at 350 degrees for 30 minutes.

Yield: 40 rolls

■ ■ ■ ■

Fresh asparagus is best from February through early June. Thinner spears are usually the most tender.

Strawberry Romaine Salad

1 cup Italian salad dressing
1/2 cup sugar
16 ounces romaine lettuce, torn into pieces
2 cups sliced fresh strawberries
1/2 cup sliced almonds

Combine the salad dressing and sugar in a bowl and mix well. Combine the lettuce and strawberries in a salad bowl. Add the almonds. Add the salad dressing and toss to mix. Serve immediately.

Yield: 8 servings

- - - -

Lettuce keeps longer stored in a paper bag than in cellophane.

South of the Border Chicken

8 boneless chicken breasts
1 teaspoon salt
1 (6-ounce) can frozen limeade concentrate, thawed
1/4 cup packed brown sugar
1 envelope fajita seasoning mix

Arrange the chicken in a single layer in a 9×13-inch baking dish. Sprinkle with the salt. Mix the undiluted concentrate, brown sugar and seasoning mix in a small bowl. Pour over the chicken. Bake, covered, at 350 degrees for 45 minutes. Bake, uncovered, for 15 minutes longer or until the chicken is cooked through.

Yield: 8 servings

- - - -

Cook a little extra on the weekends, and then enjoy the leftovers during the rest of the week.

Spanish Rice

1 cup uncooked quick-cooking brown rice
1/8 teaspoon cumin
1 1/4 cups chicken broth
1 (15-ounce) can black beans, drained
1 (4-ounce) can diced green chiles, drained

Cook the rice using the package directions, adding cumin, omitting the salt and substituting the chicken broth for water. Stir in the beans and green chiles. Cook, covered, until heated through.

Yield: 6 servings

- - - -

You can use an empty salt carton with a spout to hold bread crumbs.

Summer Squash Casserole

2 pounds yellow squash, sliced
1 large onion, chopped
2 eggs, beaten
1 cup shredded sharp Cheddar cheese
$1/3$ cup mayonnaise

Cook the squash and onion in boiling salted water in a large saucepan until tender; drain. Mash the squash and onion in the saucepan. Add the eggs, cheese and mayonnaise and mix well. Spoon into a baking dish. Bake, covered, at 350 degrees for 30 minutes.

Yield: 8 servings

- - - -

When planning a party, let your dinner guests bring an appetizer or dessert.

Almost Effortless Ice Cream Pie

10 ice cream sandwiches
1/2 cup amaretto
8 ounces milk chocolate toffee bits
1/2 cup sliced almonds
8 ounces whipped topping

Place the ice cream sandwiches in a 9×13-inch pan. Poke several holes in each sandwich. Pour half the amaretto over the sandwiches. Sprinkle with 1/2 of the toffee bits and 1/2 of the almonds. Stir the remaining 1/4 cup amaretto into the whipped topping. Spread over the sandwiches. Top with the remaining toffee bits and almonds. Freeze until serving time.

Yield: 10 servings

- - - -

Roll out pie dough between sheets of waxed paper. Sprinkle a few drops of water on the countertop first to keep the waxed paper from slipping.

Cappuccino Punch

1 quart chocolate ice cream, softened
1 quart cold coffee
2 cups fat-free half-and-half

Mix all the ingredients in a large container. Pour into a punch bowl.

Yield: 10 servings

■ ■ ■ ■ ■

Peanut Butter Fudge

2 cups (12 ounces) milk chocolate chips
1 (12-ounce) jar chunky peanut butter
1 (14-ounce) can sweetened condensed milk

Microwave the chocolate chips in a bowl on High for 2 minutes; stir. Microwave for 1 minute longer. Stir in the peanut butter and milk. Pour into an 8x8-inch pan sprayed with nonstick cooking spray. Chill until firm.

Yield: 64 pieces

■ ■ ■ ■ ■

Brickle Bit Cookies

1 (2-layer) package yellow cake mix
1/4 cup vegetable oil
1/4 cup water
1 egg
1 (10-ounce) package brickle bits

Combine the cake mix, oil, water, egg and toffee bits in a bowl and mix well. Drop by teaspoonfuls onto a greased cookie sheet. Bake at 350 degrees for 12 minutes. Cool on the cookie sheet for several minutes. Remove to a wire rack to cool completely.

Yield: 48 cookies

If you can't find brickle bits, use almond toffee bits. You can make your own brickle chips by crushing 50 almond toffee candy pieces.

Butter Pecan Brownies

1 (2-layer) package butter pecan cake mix
1/2 cup (1 stick) butter, softened
4 eggs
1 (1-pound) package confectioners' sugar
8 ounces cream cheese, softened

Combine the cake mix, butter and 1 egg in a bowl and mix well. Press over the bottom of a 9×13-inch baking pan. Cream the confectioners' sugar and cream cheese in a mixing bowl until blended and smooth. Add the remaining 3 eggs 1 at a time, beating well after each addition. Pour over the crust in the baking pan. Bake at 325 degrees for 50 minutes. Cool in the pan. Cut into squares to serve.

Yield: 12 servings

- - - -

Store these wonderful brownies in a tightly closed container. They also freeze well.

Tosh Turtle Bars

1 (12-ounce) package vanilla wafers
3/4 cup (1 1/2 sticks) butter or margarine, melted
1 2/3 cups (10 ounces) semisweet chocolate chips
1 cup pecans, chopped
1 (12-ounce) jar caramel ice cream topping

Place the vanilla wafers in a large sealable heavy-duty plastic bag. Crush to fine crumbs with a rolling pin. Mix the crumbs and butter in a bowl. Press over the bottom of a 9×13-inch baking dish. Sprinkle with the chocolate chips and pecans. Drizzle with the ice cream topping. Bake at 350 degrees for 10 to 12 minutes. Chill for 30 minutes. Cut into 1 1/2-inch squares to serve.

Yield: 4 dozen

- - - -

Take time to bake cookies or make candy with your children. Never miss an opportunity to share time with them.

Wally's Strawberry Pie

8 ounces cream cheese, softened
8 ounces whipped topping
1 teaspoon almond extract
1 (10-ounce) package frozen strawberries, thawed and drained
1 baked (9-inch) deep-dish pie shell, cooled

Beat the cream cheese and whipped topping in a mixing bowl until blended and smooth. Stir in the almond extract and strawberries. Spoon into the pie shell. Chill for 2 hours.

Yield: 8 servings

The strawberry is a member of the rose family.

Crunchy Banana Cake

4 eggs
2 large bananas, mashed
1 cup sour cream
1 (2-layer) package yellow cake mix
1 (16-ounce) can coconut pecan frosting

Combine the eggs, bananas and sour cream in a mixing
bowl and mix well. Stir in the cake mix and beat for 2 minutes. Layer
the cake batter and the frosting alternately in a greased
and floured tube pan until all the batter and frosting are used.
Bake at 325 degrees for 1 hour. Cool in the pan for
15 minutes. Invert onto a serving plate.

Yield: 12 servings

*Spoon the frosting into a microwave-safe glass
bowl and microwave it for 1 to 2 minutes to make
spreading it over the cake batter easier.*

Kay's Ambrosia

1 (11-ounce) can mandarin oranges, drained
1 (8-ounce) can pineapple tidbits, drained
4 (4-ounce) vanilla pudding snacks
12 coconut macaroons, crushed

Mix the oranges and pineapple in a bowl. Layer the fruit mixture and pudding alternately in parfait glasses. Top with the cookie crumbs.

Yield: 4 servings

– – – –

A trifle is a beautiful dessert. Serve it in a glass bowl so that all its layers can be seen.

Carley's Black Bean Dip

8 ounces cream cheese, softened
1 (15-ounce) can black beans, drained
1 (10-ounce) can tomatoes with green chiles, drained
1 cup (4 ounces) shredded Monterey Jack cheese
with jalapeños

Spread the cream cheese in a 9-inch pie plate. Layer the beans and tomatoes with chiles over the cream cheese. Top with the Monterey Jack cheese. Microwave for 2 to 3 minutes or until the cheese is melted. Serve with corn chips.

Yield: 6 servings

With only four ingredients and a spatula, you can create this beautiful appetizer in about ten minutes.

Grilled Fajitas

6 chicken breasts
1 envelope fajita seasoning mix
2 large onions, sliced
1 large bell pepper, sliced
6 large flour tortillas

Remove and discard the chicken skin and bones. Sprinkle the chicken with the seasoning mix. Grill the chicken, onions and bell pepper for 8 to 12 minutes or until the chicken is cooked through and the vegetables are tender, turning once. Chop the chicken and vegetables. Spoon the chicken and vegetables onto the tortillas and wrap to make fajitas.

Yield: 6 servings

- - - -

The grilled chicken and vegetables also make a great topper for a salad.

Southwestern Corn

2 teaspoons olive oil
1 red or green bell pepper, chopped
1/4 cup chopped onion
Kernels of 5 medium ears corn
1/4 teaspoon pepper

Heat the olive oil in a skillet. Add the bell pepper and onion and sauté until tender. Stir in the corn. Season with the pepper. Cook over low heat for 10 minutes or until the corn is tender, stirring occasionally.

Yield: 4 servings

- - - -

This is a great summer side dish—and the fresher the corn, the better the flavor.

Ann's Broccoli Slaw

1 purple onion, chopped
1 (16-ounce) bag broccoli slaw
8 slices bacon, crisp-cooked and crumbled
1 cup (4 ounces) sharp Cheddar cheese
1 cup purchased coleslaw dressing

Combine the onion, slaw, bacon and cheese in a large
salad bowl and mix well. Add the dressing and toss to coat.
Chill, covered, thoroughly before serving.

Yield: 6 servings

▬ ▬ ▬

*This coleslaw is excellent with barbecue
or grilled chicken.*

Chocolate Chip Muffins

1 (2-layer) package devil's food cake mix
1 cup water
1/2 cup vegetable oil
3 eggs
1 cup (6 ounces) chocolate chips

Combine the cake mix, water, oil and eggs in a mixing bowl.
Beat at low speed for 4 minutes. Fold in the chocolate chips. Spoon
into greased miniature muffin cups. Bake at 350 degrees for 9 minutes.
Cool in the pan for several minutes. Remove to a wire rack to cool
completely. Spread with Kahlúa Frosting (below).

Yield: 72 muffins

---

*Make Kahlúa Buttercream Frosting by beating
6 tablespoons softened unsalted butter with
2 cups sifted confectioners' sugar. Stir in 1 tablespoon
each heavy cream and Kahlúa.*

Mediterranean Dip

16 ounces feta cheese, crumbled
1 (4-ounce) can chopped black olives
1 (10-ounce) can tomatoes with green chiles
4 green onions, chopped
1 envelope Italian salad dressing mix

Combine the cheese, olives, undrained tomatoes with chiles, green onions and salad dressing mix in a bowl and mix well. Cover and chill thoroughly before serving. Serve with corn chips.

Yield: 10 servings

- - - -

During the holidays, three friends can host a progressive supper. One home can serve the appetizer, and another can host the main dish. Save house #3 for the grand finale—dessert and coffee.

Apricot Lemon Mold

2 (3-ounce) packages lemon gelatin
2 cups boiling water
1 cup sour cream
1 (8-ounce) can crushed pineapple
1 (15-ounce) can apricot halves, drained and chopped

Dissolve the gelatin in the boiling water in a bowl. Let stand for 10 minutes. Add the sour cream, pineapple and apricots and mix well. Pour into an oiled mold or a bowl. Chill until set. Unmold onto a serving plate.

Yield: 8 servings

- - - -

Add a few drops of lemon juice to boiling rice to keep the grains separate.

Lemon Garlic Salmon

1/2 **cup vegetable oil**

1 **medium onion, chopped**

2 **tablespoons lemon juice**

1 **garlic clove, minced**

2 **(1**1/2**-pound) salmon fillets**

Combine the oil, onion, lemon juice and garlic in a bowl and
mix well. Place the salmon skin side down on a broiler rack in a pan.
Broil 4 to 6 inches from the heat source for 20 minutes or
until the fish flakes easily with a fork, basting every 5 minutes with the
lemon juice mixture. Garnish with lemon slices.

Yield: 6 servings

- - - -

*With this main dish, supper will be quick,
easy, and delicious.*

Microwave Mexican Rice

2 (12-ounce) frozen corn soufflés, thawed
1¹/2 cups cooked white rice
1¹/2 cups (6 ounces) shredded sharp Cheddar cheese
1 (4-ounce) can chopped green chiles, drained
¹/4 teaspoon garlic salt

Combine the corn, rice, cheese, green chiles and garlic salt in a bowl and mix well. Spoon into a 1¹/2-quart microwave-safe dish. Microwave on High for 16 minutes, stirring once after 8 minutes.

Yield: 8 servings

- - - -

Use white candles in small crystal or glass bowls to decorate the buffet table. Arrange some candles in glasses with stems to add height and interest.

Pull-Apart Cheese Bread

24 frozen Parker House rolls, thawed
1/2 cup (1 stick) margarine, melted
1 cup bacon bits
1 cup (4 ounces) shredded Cheddar cheese
1 envelope ranch salad dressing mix

Cut each roll into 3 pieces. Combine the margarine, bacon bits, cheese and salad dressing mix in a bowl. Dip the bread into the mixture. Place the bread in an ungreased tube pan. Let rise, covered, for 2 hours. Bake at 350 degrees for 25 minutes or until golden brown.

Yield: 10 servings

- - - - -

This rich, delicious bread is a great addition to a luncheon or a tea.

Betty's Carrot Cake

1 (2-layer) package carrot cake mix
1 1/3 cups water
1/2 cup vegetable oil
3 eggs
1 (16-ounce) can coconut pecan frosting

Combine the cake mix, water, oil, eggs and frosting
(yes, the frosting) in a mixing bowl and beat for 2 minutes. Spoon
into a greased tube pan. Bake at 350 degrees for 50 minutes
or until a wooden pick inserted near the center comes out clean.
Cool in the pan. Invert onto a serving plate.

Yield: 12 servings

*This unusual cake has the frosting in the batter,
and you will love the finished product.*

Jac's Stove-Top Alfredo

1 envelope Alfredo pasta sauce mix
1 1/2 cups heavy cream
1 tablespoon olive oil
1/2 (6-ounce) package frozen mixed onions and bell peppers
2 chicken breasts, cooked and chopped

Combine the pasta sauce mix and cream in a bowl and blend well. Heat the olive oil in a skillet. Add the mixed vegetables and sauté briefly. Add the chicken and mix well. Pour the Alfredo sauce over the chicken. Cook until heated through and bubbly. Serve over pasta.

Yield: 4 servings

You will have a head start on your Sunday night supper by substituting prepared pasta sauce or a jar of Alfredo sauce.

Guckert Chicken Olé

6 chicken breasts, deboned and cooked
1 (10-ounce) can tomatoes with green chiles
2 (10-ounce) cans cream of mushroom soup
8 ounces sharp Cheddar cheese, grated
1 (12-ounce) package corn chips

Arrange the chicken in a single layer in a 9×13-inch baking dish. Mix the tomatoes with chiles and undiluted soup in a bowl. Spoon half the mixture over the chicken. Top with half the cheese and half the corn chips. Repeat the process with the remaining tomato mixture, cheese and corn chips. Bake at 350 degrees for 30 minutes.

Yield: 6 servings

- - - -

Encourage your children to learn how to cook a one-dish meal.

Shrimp Montgomery

1/2 cup (1 stick) butter
1 pound fresh shrimp, peeled and rinsed
1 (10-ounce) can cream of mushroom soup
1 (5-ounce) jar Old English cheese spread
1 (12-ounce) package egg noodles, cooked and drained

Melt the butter in a saucepan. Add the shrimp. Cook for
5 minutes or until the shrimp turn pink, stirring frequently. Add the
undiluted soup, cheese and noodles and mix well.
Cook until heated through.

Yield: 4 servings

- - - -

*Add two drops of yellow food coloring to boiling
noodles to make them look homemade.*

Pork Chops Dianne

4 boneless pork chops
1 teaspoon salt
1 tablespoon Worcestershire sauce
1 tablespoon olive oil
1 (14-ounce) can diced tomatoes with bell peppers,
onions and celery

Sprinkle the pork chops with the salt and Worcestershire sauce. Heat the olive oil in a skillet. Add the pork chops. Cook until brown on both sides. Add the tomatoes and mix well. Cook, covered, for 30 minutes or until the pork chops are cooked through. Serve over rice.

Yield: 4 servings

- - - -

*Add a packaged salad and garlic bread
for a classic Italian meal.*

Artichoke Quiche

3 eggs
1 cup (4 ounces) shredded 6-cheese Italian blend
1 (14-ounce) can artichoke hearts, drained and chopped
3/4 stick pepperoni, thinly sliced
1 unbaked (9-inch) pie shell

Beat the eggs with the cheese in a mixing bowl. Add the
artichoke hearts and pepperoni and mix well. Pour into the pie shell.
Bake at 375 degrees for 45 minutes.

Yield: 6 servings

- - - -

*Typical Italian blends include mozzarella, provolone,
Parmesan, Romano, fontina, and asiago cheeses.*

Take 5... Menus of Fall

Football Tailgate Party

- - - -

Harvest Dinner

- - - -

Simple Pasta Supper

The Thanksgiving Feast

- - - -

Lazy Day Breakfast

- - - -

Happy Birthday Dinner

- - - -

Fast-Lane Dinners for Fall

Green Olive Spread

1 cup green olives
8 ounces cream cheese, softened
1/2 cup mayonnaise
1/2 cup pecan chips

Drain the olives, reserving 2 teaspoons juice. Chop the olives.
Mix the cream cheese, mayonnaise and reserved juice in a bowl.
Stir in the pecans and olives. Serve with wheat crackers.

Yield: 2 cups

— — — —

*For Waltman Taco Dip, layer 9 ounces bean dip,
6 ounces guacamole, 1 cup sour cream, 16 ounces
chunky salsa, and 2 cups Cheddar cheese 1/2 at a time
on a platter. Serve with chips. Makes 12 servings.*

Merrie's Apple Dip

8 ounces cream cheese, softened
3/4 cup packed brown sugar
1 tablespoon vanilla extract

Combine the cream cheese, brown sugar and vanilla in a bowl and mix well. Serve with sliced apples.

Yield: 1 1/2 cups

- - - -

Did you know that apple pie came to this country from England with the Pilgrims?

Shrimp Dip Hannah Beth

1 (8-ounce) container French onion dip
8 ounces cream cheese, softened
1/4 cup lemon juice
1/4 teaspoon cayenne pepper
1 (2-ounce) can small shrimp, drained

Combine the onion dip, cream cheese, lemon juice
and cayenne pepper in a bowl and mix well. Stir in the shrimp.
Serve with corn chips.

Yield: 8 servings

■ ■ ■ ■

*This dip is always a crowd-pleaser. Stir in one
14-ounce can of drained, chopped artichoke
hearts for Artichoke Shrimp Dip.*

Laurie's Artichoke and Spinach Dip

2 (10-ounce) packages frozen creamed spinach,
thawed and drained
1 cup (4 ounces) grated Parmesan cheese
2 to 3 cups (8 to 12 ounces) shredded Monterey Jack cheese
1 (14-ounce) can chopped artichoke hearts, drained

Mix the spinach, Parmesan cheese, most of the Monterey Jack cheese and the artichoke hearts in a bowl. Spoon into a baking dish. Sprinkle with the remaining Monterey Jack cheese. Bake at 350 degrees for 30 minutes. Serve with tortilla chips, sour cream and salsa.

Yield: 8 servings

- - - -

Make Cheese and Corn Dip by mixing 3 cups shredded sharp Cheddar cheese, 1/2 cup sour cream, 1 can of Mexican-style corn, 1/2 cup mayonnaise, and 1 tablespoon onion flakes. Serve with crackers or fresh vegetables. Makes 3 cups.

Cheesy Bacon Swirls

5 slices bacon, crisp-cooked and crumbled
3 ounces cream cheese, softened
1/4 cup finely chopped onion
1 teaspoon milk
1 (8-count) can refrigerator crescent rolls

Mix the first 4 ingredients in a bowl. Unroll the crescent roll dough without separating along the ridges. Roll into an 8×15-inch rectangle, pressing the perforations to seal. Spread the cheese mixture evenly over the dough, leaving a 1/2-inch margin at each edge. Beginning with a long side, roll up as for a jelly roll; press the perforations again to seal. Cut the roll into 1/2-inch slices. Place cut side down on an ungreased baking sheet. Bake at 375 degrees for 14 minutes.

Yield: 30 servings

- - - -

Buy a box of white freezer paper at the grocery store. Your family will enjoy making banners to say "HAPPY BIRTHDAY" or "WELCOME HOME"!

Hayley's Brownies

1 (21-ounce) package brownie mix
2 eggs
1/2 cup vegetable oil
1/4 cup water
1 (7-ounce) Symphony candy bar, broken into small pieces

Mix the first 4 ingredients in a large bowl just until moistened. Pour half the mixture into a greased 8×8-inch baking pan. Sprinkle with the candy. Cover with the remaining batter. Bake at 350 degrees for 42 minutes. Cool in the pan before cutting into squares.

Yield: 12 servings

■ ■ ■ ■

For Light-as-Air Cookies, beat 3 egg whites in a mixer bowl until stiff peaks form. Add 1/2 cup sugar gradually, beating constantly. Stir in 1/2 cup packed brown sugar and 1 1/2 cups chopped pecans. Drop by spoonfuls onto a greased cookie sheet. Bake at 275 degrees for 35 minutes. Cool on the cookie sheet for several minutes. Remove to a wire rack to cool completely. Makes 36 cookies.

Double D Cookie Bars

1/2 cup (1 stick) margarine, melted
1 1/2 cups graham cracker crumbs
1 (14-ounce) can sweetened condensed milk
2 cups (12 ounces) semisweet chocolate chips
1 cup (6 ounces) peanut butter chips

Pour the margarine into a 9×13-inch baking pan. Sprinkle the graham cracker crumbs over the margarine. Pour the condensed milk over the graham cracker crumbs. Top with the chocolate chips and peanut butter chips. Press the chips down firmly. Bake at 350 degrees for 25 minutes. Cool in the pan before cutting into bars.

Yield: 24 bars

Try these wonderful cookies for a crisp-yet-chewy snack. They make a great after-school treat or bedtime snack.

Joy's Potato Soup

2 tablespoons margarine
1$1/2$ cups chopped green onions
2 cups sliced peeled potatoes
2$1/2$ cups chicken broth
1 cup milk

Melt the margarine in a large saucepan. Add the green onions and simmer for 5 minutes. Add the potatoes and chicken broth and mix well. Simmer for 30 minutes, stirring occasionally. Add the milk and stir briskly.

Yield: 6 servings

▬ ▬ ▬ ▬

Make an "I care for you" basket for a sick friend. Line the basket with a colorful napkin and place a container of homemade soup and a fun magazine inside. Soup is a great comfort food.

Thai Chicken

1 (6-ounce) can frozen lemonade concentrate, thawed
1 cup chunky peanut butter
1/2 cup soy sauce
1/2 teaspoon cayenne pepper
4 boneless chicken breasts

Combine the lemonade concentrate, peanut butter, soy sauce and cayenne pepper in a sealable plastic bag. Add the chicken. Seal the bag and turn several times to coat the chicken. Drain the chicken, discarding the marinade. Grill the chicken over medium heat for 4 minutes per side or until cooked through.

Yield: 4 servings

- - - -

Off-white candles of all shapes and sizes in glass containers add a beautiful, warm glow to a fall tablescape. Weave vines of bittersweet and autumn leaves down the center of the table. Tuck in small pumpkins and gourds.

Quick Spinach and Artichoke Casserole

2 (10-ounce) packages frozen chopped spinach
1 (14-ounce) can artichoke hearts, drained
8 ounces cream cheese, softened
1/2 cup (1 stick) butter, softened
1 (8-ounce) can water chestnuts, drained and chopped

Cook the spinach using the package directions; drain. Cut the artichoke hearts into halves and arrange in a 9×9-inch baking dish. Combine the spinach, cream cheese, butter and water chestnuts in a bowl and mix well. Spoon over the artichoke hearts. Bake at 350 degrees for 20 minutes or until heated through.

Yield: 6 servings

- - - -

A simple supper buffet is a great way to entertain. The host can enjoy the meal instead of being stuck in the kitchen.

Crisp Salad with Balsamic Vinaigrette

3 tablespoons balsamic vinegar

2 tablespoons sugar

$1/4$ cup olive oil

1 teaspoon dry mustard

$1/2$ teaspoon seasoned salt

Mix the vinegar, sugar, olive oil, mustard and seasoned salt in a bowl. Serve over torn crisp romaine lettuce.

Yield: 4 servings

- - - -

For McDade Muffins, combine 3 cups baking mix, 1 pound fully cooked sausage, 1 undiluted 10-ounce can Cheddar cheese soup, 1/2 cup water, and 1 cup shredded sharp Cheddar cheese in a bowl and mix well. Spoon into greased miniature muffin cups. Bake at 400 degrees for 15 minutes. Makes 36 muffins.

Chocolate Torte

1 roll refrigerator peanut butter cookie dough
12 ounces cream cheese, softened
6 (4-ounce) chocolate pudding snacks
8 ounces whipped topping
1/2 cup (3 ounces) miniature chocolate chips

Press the cookie dough onto a round pizza pan. Bake at
375 degrees for 15 minutes. Beat the cream cheese in a mixing bowl
until smooth. Spread over the crust. Spread the pudding over the
cream cheese. Top with the whipped topping. Sprinkle with the
chocolate chips. Chill thoroughly before serving.

Yield: 12 servings

■ ■ ■ ■

*Everybody's favorite cookie is adapted
for this dessert pizza. You can prepare the
crust the day before.*

Black Bean Dip

2 (15-ounce) cans black beans, drained
1 (9-ounce) container Cheddar jalapeño dip
1 bunch green onions, chopped
1 tablespoon chopped cilantro
1 tomato, chopped

Purée the beans in a blender. Combine the puréed beans, cheese dip, green onions, cilantro and tomato in a mixing bowl and mix well. Serve with tortilla chips.

Yield: 3 cups

To peel a fresh tomato, drop the whole tomato into boiling water and boil for 1 minute. Remove the tomato from the water, and the peel will slip right off.

Sara's Cheesy Ravioli

1 (24-ounce) package frozen ravioli
1 (26-ounce) jar spaghetti sauce
2 cups cottage cheese
16 ounces mozzarella cheese, shredded
16 ounces Cheddar cheese, shredded

Cook the ravioli using the package directions; drain. Layer the spaghetti sauce, ravioli, cottage cheese, mozzarella cheese and Cheddar cheese $1/2$ at a time in a 9×13-inch baking dish. Bake at 350 degrees for 40 minutes.

Yield: 6 servings

- - - -

Let your children make this casserole and place it in the freezer as a gift to Mom. Double the recipe and have one for supper and the other for a particularly busy day.

Parmesan Asparagus

1 pound fresh asparagus
1/4 cup Italian salad dressing
1/2 cup (2 ounces) grated Parmesan cheese

Snap off the tough ends of the asparagus. Peel the stalks if desired. Place the asparagus in the center of an 18×24-inch sheet of heavy-duty foil. Drizzle with the salad dressing. Sprinkle with the cheese. Fold the opposite edges of the foil together over the asparagus. Crimp and fold the remaining edges to seal. Place on oven rack. Bake at 375 degrees for 30 minutes.

Yield: 4 servings

This Italian dish has taken on a new look.

Dijon Breadsticks

1 envelope Italian salad dressing mix
1/4 cup Dijon mustard
1 tablespoon grated Parmesan cheese
3 tablespoons margarine or butter, softened
1 (12-count) package refrigerator soft breadsticks

Combine the salad dressing mix, Dijon mustard, cheese and margarine in a bowl and mix well. Unroll the breadstick dough and cut crosswise into halves. Cut each piece into halves lengthwise. Separate the strips and twist each slightly. Place on baking sheets. Brush generously with the mustard mixture. Bake at 350 degrees for 15 minutes or until light brown.

Yield: 6 servings

— — — —

When the supper club meets at your house, top off the meal with two or three desserts. Your guests will love the choices.

Presenting . . . Deli Cheesecake

1 (18- to 28-ounce) plain deli cheesecake
1 (21-ounce) can blueberry pie filling
1 (21-ounce) can cherry pie filling
1 (12-ounce) jar chocolate ice cream topping
2 cups chopped pecans or walnuts

Place the cheesecake on a serving plate. Cut into 12 slices. Place each of the toppings in a separate bowl. Top each slice of cheesecake as desired.

Yield: 12 servings

■ ■ ■ ■

This cheesecake buffet will remind you of an old-fashioned church ice cream social. Make sure you have extra plates, because some guests will want to go back for seconds. (And you might want to dispose of the deli box, too.)

Corn Chowder

1/4 cup chopped onion
1 quart milk
4 cups cubed peeled potatoes
1 chicken bouillon cube
2 (16-ounce) cans cream-style corn

Brng the onion, milk, potatoes and bouillon cube to a boil in a large saucepan. Boil for 20 minutes or until the potatoes are tender. Stir in the corn. Cook for 10 minutes.

Yield: 6 servings

- - - -

For Frosty Cherry Salad, combine one 21-ounce can cherry pie filling, 16 ounces whipped topping, 2 cups miniature marshmallows, 1 drained 20-ounce can crushed pineapple, and one 14-ounce can sweetened condensed milk in a bowl and mix well. Spoon into a 9×13-inch freezer-proof dish and freeze. Remove from the freezer 20 minutes before serving. Makes 8 servings.

Holiday Glazed Ham

1/2 cup packed brown sugar

1 teaspoon dry mustard

1 teaspoon prepared horseradish

1/4 cup Coca-Cola, Pepsi or other cola-flavored soda

1 (5- to 6-pound) boneless smoked ham

Combine the brown sugar, mustard, horseradish and half the soda in a bowl and mix well. Rub over the ham. Place the ham in a 5-quart slow cooker. Pour the remaining soda over the ham. Cook, covered, on low for 8 to 10 hours or until a meat thermometer inserted into the thickest portion of the ham registers 160 degrees.

Yield: 15 to 20 servings

- - - -

Use a pumpkin (with pulp and seeds removed) to hold fresh flowers for a Thanksgiving Day centerpiece. Small pots of mums will last about a week.

Vera's Oven-Roasted Sweet Potatoes

4 medium sweet potatoes, peeled and cut into 2-inch pieces
2 medium Vidalia onions or other sweet onions, sliced
2 tablespoons extra-virgin olive oil
3/4 teaspoon garlic pepper blend
1/2 teaspoon salt

Combine the sweet potatoes, onions, olive oil, garlic pepper blend and salt in a bowl and mix well to coat the vegetables with olive oil. Spoon into a 9×13-inch baking dish. Bake at 425 degrees for 35 minutes or until the vegetables are tender, stirring occasionally.

Yield: 6 servings

You can substitute new potatoes or red-skinned potatoes for the sweet potatoes in this recipe.

Frank's Green Beans

6 slices bacon, cut into small pieces
2 (14-ounce) cans green beans, drained
2 to 4 tablespoons Worcestershire sauce
2 to 3 dashes Tabasco sauce, or to taste

Brown the bacon in a saucepan; drain, returning some of the drippings to the saucepan with the bacon. Add the green beans, Worcestershire sauce and Tabasco sauce and mix well. Cook until heated through, stirring occasionally.

Yield: 6 servings

For One-Step Mac and Cheese, combine 1 cup uncooked macaroni, 1 cup shredded Velveeta cheese, one 16-ounce can cream-style corn, 1 undrained 15-ounce can whole kernel corn, and 1/2 cup melted margarine in a bowl and mix well. Spoon into a baking dish. Bake, covered, at 350 degrees for 30 minutes. Bake, uncovered, for 30 minutes longer.

Perfect Pumpkin Pie

1 (15-ounce) can pumpkin
1 (14-ounce) can sweetened condensed milk
2 eggs
1 teaspoon apple pie spice
1 (9-inch) graham cracker pie shell

Combine the pumpkin, condensed milk, eggs and apple pie spice in a mixing bowl and beat until blended and smooth. Spoon into the pie shell. Bake at 425 degrees for 15 minutes. Reduce the oven temperature to 350 degrees. Bake for 35 to 40 minutes longer or until a knife inserted near the center comes out clean. Let cool before slicing. Garnish as desired. Store leftovers in the refrigerator.

Yield: 8 servings

A quick twist on a traditional holiday pie.

Cheese Muffins

2 cups baking mix

1 egg, beaten

1 cup milk

$1/4$ cup ($1/2$ stick) butter, melted

$1 1/2$ cups (6 ounces) shredded sharp Cheddar cheese

Combine the baking mix, egg, milk, butter and cheese in a bowl and mix well. Spoon into greased muffin cups. Bake at 425 degrees for 20 minutes. Cool in the pan for several minutes. Remove to a wire rack to cool completely.

Yield: 12 muffins

- - - -

To prepare Jana's Cranberry Bake, layer 2 cups fresh or thawed frozen cranberries, one 21-ounce can apple pie filling, $1 1/2$ cups rolled oats, and $1/2$ cup packed brown sugar in a baking dish. Top with $1/2$ cup margarine, cut into pats. Bake at 300 degrees for 1 hour. Top with chopped nuts to add a little crunch. Makes 10 servings.

McKay Hash Brown Casserole

1 (32-ounce) package frozen hash brown potatoes
1 (10-ounce) can cream of chicken soup
12 ounces sharp Cheddar cheese, shredded
1 cup sour cream
1/2 cup chopped onion

Combine the potatoes, undiluted soup, cheese, sour cream and onion in a bowl and mix well. Spoon into a baking dish. Bake at 350 degrees for 30 minutes or until heated through.

Yield: 8 servings

- - - -

Your overnight guests will love getting up to share this "big" breakfast with you. You can prepare it days ahead and freeze it.

Cream Cheese Danish Pinwheels

8 ounces cream cheese, softened
1/2 cup sugar
2 (8-count) cans refrigerator crescent rolls
1 cup fresh blueberries (optional)
1 cup chopped pecans

Beat the cream cheese and sugar in a mixing bowl until blended and smooth. Unroll both cans of roll dough and shape each into a rectangle on a floured surface. Press the perforations to seal. Spread half the cream cheese mixture on each rectangle. Sprinkle each with half the blueberries and pecans. Roll up each rectangle as for a jelly roll and cut into 12 to 16 slices. Place on a baking sheet. Bake at 350 degrees for 15 minutes or until light brown.

Yield: 8 servings

Make a Sunday night ritual of preparing omelets or French toast with your children.

Brickle Bread

1 (2-layer) package butter pecan cake mix
1 (3-ounce) package toasted coconut
pudding mix or coconut cream pudding mix
4 eggs
1 cup hot water
1/4 cup vegetable oil

Combine the cake mix, pudding mix, eggs, hot water and oil in a bowl and mix well. Pour half the batter into each of two 5×9-inch loaf pans. Bake at 350 degrees for 45 minutes or until golden brown.

Yield: 12 servings

- - - -

This bread is even better if you add 2 cups chopped pecans to the batter.

Monterey Shrimp Dip

8 ounces Monterey Jack cheese with jalapeños, shredded
2 (4-ounce) cans shrimp, drained
1 (2-ounce) can sliced black olives, drained
3/4 cup mayonnaise
1/4 cup chopped green onions

Combine the cheese, shrimp, olives, mayonnaise and green onions in a 1-quart microwave-safe dish. Microwave on High for 3 minutes or until the cheese is melted. Serve with tortilla chips.

Yield: 6 servings

▬ ▬ ▬ ▬

Start your next party with this zesty shrimp dip. It is always a crowd-pleaser.

Moroccan Chicken

8 large skinless chicken breasts
1 tablespoon lemon pepper
1 (7-ounce) jar sun-dried tomatoes in olive oil
1 (6-ounce) jar marinated artichoke hearts
2 cups chicken broth (not low-fat)

Arrange the chicken in a single layer in a 9×13-inch baking dish. Sprinkle with the lemon pepper. Top with the undrained tomatoes and undrained artichoke hearts. Pour the chicken broth over the top. Bake, covered, at 350 degrees for 45 minutes. Uncover the baking dish and bake for 30 minutes longer. Serve over saffron rice.

Yield: 8 servings

- - - -

Wrap birthday gifts in brightly colored paper, and place them in the center of the table. Tie helium-filled balloons to each gift to complete the centerpiece. Use colorful party hats as place card holders.

Tarragon Carrots

12 to 14 carrots, sliced diagonally
2 teaspoons instant chicken bouillon
2 tablespoons sugar
2 teaspoons butter or margarine
1/2 teaspoon tarragon

Combine the carrots, bouillon granules and sugar in a medium saucepan. Cook, covered, until the carrots are tender-crisp. Drain the liquid from the saucepan. Stir the butter and tarragon gently into the carrots.

Yield: 4 servings

- - - -

For Cranberry Apple Salad, combine three 8-ounce bags lettuce, 1 cup chopped pecans or walnuts, 1 cup sweetened dried cranberries, and 3 chopped small red apples in a large salad bowl. Add one 8-ounce bottle vinaigrette salad dressing and toss to coat. Makes 8 servings.

Key Lime Pies

3 egg yolks
2/3 cup fresh lime juice
2 (14-ounce) cans sweetened condensed milk
2 (9-inch) graham cracker pie shells
1 cup whipped topping

Combine the egg yolks, lime juice and condensed milk in a bowl and mix well. Pour into the pie shells. Bake at 350 degrees for 15 minutes. Chill for 2 hours. Top with whipped topping just before serving.

Yield: 12 servings

- - - -

To prepare Mayonnaise Biscuits, mix 1 cup self-rising flour, 1/8 teaspoon salt, and 1/4 cup sugar in a bowl. Stir in 3 tablespoons mayonnaise and 1/2 cup milk. Drop by spoonfuls into buttered muffin cups and bake at 400 degrees for 12 minutes. Makes 6 servings.

Encore Turkey Pie

1 (10-ounce) can cream of chicken soup
2 cups chopped cooked turkey
1 1/4 cups baking mix
1/2 cup milk
1 egg

Combine the undiluted soup and turkey in a bowl and mix well.
Spoon into a 9-inch pie plate. Combine the baking mix,
milk and egg in a bowl and mix well. Pour over the turkey
mixture. Bake at 400 degrees for 30 minutes.

Yield: 4 servings

----

*Let your children invite one or two friends over to cook.
Help them make this casserole and let them spoon it
into disposable aluminum pie plates. They will have fun
cooking, but will have even more fun surprising their
moms and dads. This is also a good holiday project
for your Scout troops or church groups.*

Chicken Bertagna

1/3 **cup olive oil**
2 **garlic cloves, minced**
6 **chicken breast fillets**
1/2 **pound Italian sausage, casing removed**
2 **(14-ounce) cans chunky Italian tomatoes**

Heat the olive oil in a skillet. Add the garlic and sauté briefly. Add the chicken fillets and sausage and cook until brown. Pour into a 9×13-inch baking dish. Bake at 350 degrees for 15 minutes. Remove from the oven and top with the tomatoes. Bake for 10 minutes longer. Serve over yellow rice. Garnish with black olives.

Yield: 6 servings

■ ■ ■ ■

This spectacular entrée will fit well into your busy schedule. It is easy and quick to make and can be frozen ahead of time.

Pork Roast

1 (4-pound) pork butt roast
1/3 cup Worcestershire sauce
3/4 cup packed light brown sugar
1 cup apple juice
1/2 teaspoon salt

Preheat the oven to 400 degrees. Place the pork in a casserole just large enough to hold it. Use a casserole with an ovenproof lid. Sprinkle the Worcestershire sauce over the roast. Coat all sides with brown sugar, pressing the brown sugar into the roast. Pour the apple juice into the casserole. Place in the oven and decrease the oven temperature to 200 degrees. Without opening the oven, bake, covered, for 5 hours or until the roast is tender and cooked through.

Yield: 8 servings

For a fall centerpiece, fill a small melon basket or brightly colored mixing bowl with fresh gourds and small pumpkins. Fresh yellow or green squash will also add a dash of color. This easy tablescape will last for two weeks.

Salmon Patties

1 (7-ounce) can pink salmon, drained
1 cup bread crumbs
2 eggs, beaten
1/2 cup chopped onion
2 tablespoons vegetable oil

Combine the salmon, bread crumbs, eggs and onion in a bowl and mix well. Shape into 4 patties. Heat the oil in a nonstick skillet over medium-high heat. Cook the salmon in the hot oil for 2 minutes or until brown on 1 side. Turn the patties and reduce the heat to medium. Cook for 5 minutes.

Yield: 4 servings

It takes about four slices of bread to yield one cup of bread crumbs.

Hearty Quiche

1 pound ground beef
1 unbaked (9-inch) pie shell
1 cup (4 ounces) shredded sharp Cheddar cheese
3 eggs
1 cup heavy cream

Brown the ground beef in a skillet, stirring until crumbly; drain well. Spoon into the pie shell. Sprinkle with the cheese. Beat the eggs and cream in a bowl until blended and smooth. Pour over the cheese. Bake at 350 degrees for 30 minutes or until a knife inserted near the center comes out clean.

Yield: 6 to 8 servings

For easier shredding, spray the cheese grater with nonstick cooking spray.

Contributors

Gwen Anderson

Wayne Andrews

Juanita Body

Sara Brashier

Debbie Campbell

Betty Case

Caroline Castle

Patsy Castle

Paula Chance

Kristen Dabbs

Ruth Dabbs

Sarah Jo Dabbs

Trent Dabbs

Nancy Farrar

Janice Guckert

Barbara Glen

Teena Grantham

Carmen Hammack

Carley Jackson

Christopher Jacobs

Hannah Beth Jacobs

Wally Kennedy

Betsy Kimbriel

Beth Long

Jane McGee

Wendy McKay

Larry Miller

Jan Moncrief

Ginger Montgomery

Freddie Montgomery

Frank Montgomery

Stacy Neal

Adrienne Patton

Tricia Randall

Christine Rayburn

Hayley Roberts

Jennie Roberts

Margaret Roberts

Dianne Robinson

Frances Robinson

Jaclyn Robinson

Joe Shelton

Joy Shelton

Jana Smith

Katherine Bell Speed

Pam Stroble

Betty Sullivan

Helen Thompson

Sally Thompson

Kay Van Skiver

Harriett Waltman

Brenda Watts

Sue Watts

Laurie Wiley

Merrie Wiley

Pearl Wiley

Vera Williams

Ann Wright

Formal Dinner

The tablecloth should be lace or linen and should hang 9 to 15 inches over the table edge on each side. Fold napkins once the long way and twice the short way to form a rectangle as shown below. (Diners place their napkins in their laps as soon as they are seated.) Use silver, not stainless steel, for formal occasions, and place it about 1 inch from the table edge; allow about 24 inches of dining space per person. Diners use the pieces on the outside first, working their way in as the meal progresses. If the salad will be served before dinner or if it replaces the fish course, rearrange the knives and forks accordingly. Utensils, plates, and glasses for each course are cleared at the end of that course, so that only the water glass remains on the table after the meat course. The dessert course may instead be laid and served separately. Servers present items from the left and clear them from the right.

1. Fish fork
2. Meat fork
3. Salad fork
4. Service plate
5. Napkin
6. Salad knife
7. Meat knife
8. Fish knife
9. Soup spoon
10. Dessert fork
11. Dessert spoon
12. White wine glass
13. Red wine glass
14. Sherry glass
15. Water glass
16. Place card

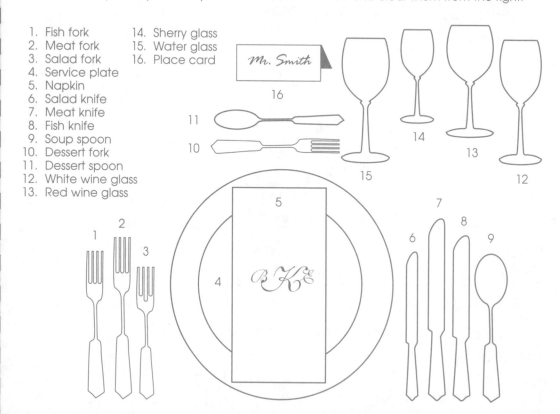

Informal Dinner

■ ■ ■ ■ ■

The informal dinner setting varies according to the number and types of courses.
The basic setting when the guests gather is illustrated below. Reverse the positions of the
salad knife and fork if the salad is served before dinner. Do not lay the implements
for soup and appetizer courses if those courses will not be served.
For family-style service, pass food around the table to the right.

1. Napkin
2. Dinner fork
3. Salad fork
4. Dinner plate
5. Appetizer
6. Salad knife
7. Dinner knife
8. Soup spoon
9. Appetizer fork
10. Bread plate
11. Butter knife
12. Water glass
13. Wine glass

Buffet

Buffet guests eat at small tables, around a large table, or just scattered throughout the room or rooms in which the party is being held. Generally, food, dishes, silver, napkins, and coffee are arrayed on a large table. Guests help themselves, beginning by picking up a plate and proceeding clockwise around the table, ending with the silver and napkin. If the buffet table is against one wall, the coffee, cups, cream, sugar, silver, and napkins can be set up at a smaller table. Guests return to the original table for dessert or go to another buffet table that has been set up for dessert.

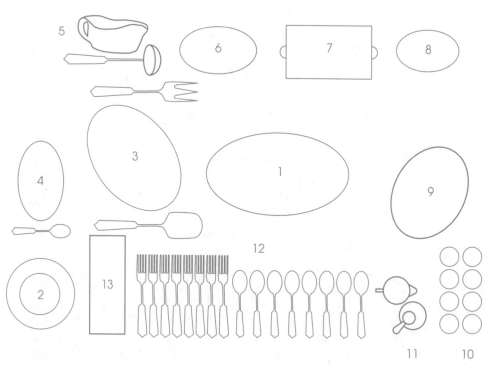

1. Centerpiece
2. Plates
3. Main dish
4. Vegetable
5. Gravy
6. Vegetable
7. Rolls
8. Relish plate
9. Coffee service
10. Cups
11. Cream, sugar, and spoon
12. Silver
13. Napkins

Buffet or Picnic Napkin Fold

With napkin open to full size, fold in half, bringing up the left side from the bottom (Illus. 1).
Fold in half again on dotted line, bringing up right side from bottom.
Four points are at top (Illus. 2). Roll down top layer (Illus. 3). Fold opposite corners under (Illus. 4).
Insert silverware into pocket (Illus. 5).

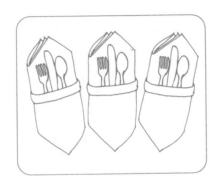

Illustration 2

Illustration 3

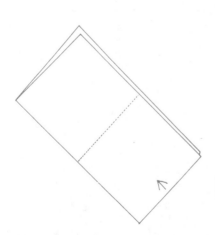

Illustration 1

Illustration 4

Illustration 5

Baking Equivalents

When the recipe calls for . . . . **Use**

Baking

1/2 cup (1 stick) butter . . . . 4 ounces
2 cups (4 sticks) butter . . . . 1 pound
4 cups all-purpose flour . . . . 1 pound
4 1/2 cups sifted cake flour . . . . 1 pound
1 square chocolate . . . . 1 ounce
1 cup semisweet chocolate chips . . . . 6 ounces
4 cups marshmallows . . . . 1 pound
2 1/4 cups packed brown sugar . . . . 1 pound
4 cups confectioners' sugar . . . . 1 pound
2 cups sugar . . . . 1 pound

Cereal/Bread

1 cup fine dry bread crumbs . . . . 4 to 5 slices
1 cup soft bread crumbs . . . . 2 slices
1 cup small bread crumbs . . . . 2 slices
1 cup fine saltine crumbs . . . . 28 saltines
1 cup fine graham cracker crumbs . . . . 15 graham crackers
1 cup vanilla wafer crumbs . . . . 22 wafers
1 cup crushed cornflakes . . . . 3 cups uncrushed
4 cups cooked macaroni . . . . 8 ounces uncooked
3 1/2 cups cooked rice . . . . 1 cup uncooked

Dairy

1 cup shredded cheese . . . . 4 ounces
1 cup cottage cheese . . . . 8 ounces
1 cup sour cream . . . . 8 ounces
1 cup whipped cream . . . . 1/2 cup heavy cream
2/3 cup evaporated milk . . . . 1 (5 1/3-ounce) can
1 2/3 cups evaporated milk . . . . 1 (13-ounce) can

Fruit

4 cups sliced or chopped apples . . . . 4 medium
1 cup mashed bananas . . . . 3 medium
2 cups pitted cherries . . . . 4 cups unpitted
2 1/2 cups shredded coconut . . . . 8 ounces
4 cups cranberries . . . . 1 pound
1 cup pitted dates . . . . 1 (8-ounce) package
1 cup candied fruit . . . . 1 (8-ounce) package
3 to 4 tablespoons lemon juice plus . . . . 1 lemon
    1 tablespoon grated lemon peel
1/3 cup orange juice plus 2 teaspoons grated orange peel . . . . 1 orange
4 cups sliced peaches . . . . 8 medium
2 cups pitted prunes . . . . 1 (12-ounce) package
3 cups raisins . . . . 1 (15-ounce) package

Index

Take Five Cookbooks

117 Muscadine Hill
Madison, Mississippi 39110

Name

Street Address

City   State   Zip

	Qty.	Total
Take Five, A Holiday Cookbook $18.95 per book		$
Take Five, For Every Occasion $18.95 per book		$
Other cookbooks available from Debbye Dabbs		
Take Five, A Cookbook $12 per book		$
Take Five, A Light Cookbook $12 per book		$
Beyond the Grill, A Cookbook for Men $12 per book		$
Shipping and Handling		
$3.00 per book, includes sales tax		$
Total		$

Please make checks payable to Take Five Cookbooks.

About the Author

Debbye Dabbs is the author of six cookbooks with five ingredients or less. A Mississippi native, Dabbs is a graduate of the University of Southern Mississippi with a degree in lower elementary education. She is married to former classmate Kelly, and they have two children.

A self-published author, Dabbs leads seminars, gives lectures, and travels the country speaking on cooking simple meals for busy families. Take Five recipes are featured monthly in the *Jackson Christian Family* magazine.